To s(

https

GW00601970

Praise for *Walk It Out: Embracing Your Destiny in Difficult Times*

"*Walk It Out* will allow readers to witness the beauty displayed when faith and life intersect."

Dan Rutty
Worship Pastor of Southbrook Church
Wesley Chapel, North Carolina

"With every reason not to be, Kelly Tyler is the most positive person you will ever meet. Her book, *Walk It Out*, will invade and challenge the impossible, and encourage the reader to believe that God can take tragedy and turn it into triumph. To many lives plagued with hopelessness and despair, this book is a ray of hope that can make any day a new day and give faith to face any difficulty."

Dr. Joe L. Fauss
President and International Director of Calvary Commission

Walk It Out

Walk It Out

Embracing Your Destiny in Difficult Times

by Kelly Tyler

TATE PUBLISHING & *Enterprises*

Published by Tate Publishing & Enterprises, LLC
127 E. Trade Center Terrace | Mustang, Oklahoma 73064 USA
1.888.361.9473 | www.tatepublishing.com

Tate Publishing is committed to excellence in the publishing industry. The company reflects the philosophy established by the founders, based on Psalm 68:11,
"The Lord gave the word and great was the company of those who published it."

Book design copyright © 2008 by Tate Publishing, LLC. All rights reserved.
Cover & Interior design by Jacob Crissup

Published in the United States of America

ISBN: 978-1-60604-941-9
1. Inspirational Autobiography, Spiritual Journey
2. Faith, Paralysis
08.09.03

To the Bride

Be encouraged and strengthened;
Rise up and go forth in power.

Acknowledgements

Thanks to my friend Dianne Tarlton, who unwittingly gave me the title of this book by her unmoving faith and constant exhortation to "just walk it out."

Thanks to my friend Dr. Ingrid Buch-Wagler, for all her help and feedback, but most of all for believing in this project.

To my daughter, Alexa, who went to the bookstore with me as I wrote the first several chapters. You made some of the most difficult parts to write a delightful memory. You were better than a personal muse!

To my son Joshua, who through thick and thin has never, ever given up on me walking!

To Josiah, you are a promise and a symbol of hope.

I would never have made it this far without all your hugs!

Ry, thanks for the last twenty years. You're my best friend ever, and I'm in love with you!

Table of Contents

Foreword

This life is a journey beyond a sequence of chronological events, jobs, contests, and the usual gamut of earthly whims and woes. For those who have been exposed to the light, it is a living tapestry of encounters.

It has been my honor to speak to and meet people on five continents. Some relationships are real show stoppers and take you into a zone of deeper understanding. Such is the case of Kelly Tyler; her husband, Ryan; and their family who are walking out a life with unthinkable obstacles. Already, their victories put them in my hall of fame of "Holy Heroes."

I reckon it's going on twelve years since our mutual friend brought us together. I had just concluded speaking at a crowded conference in a tight but warm building near Akron, Ohio when somebody jostled me as I tried to gracefully exit the clogged entryway. "Could you please pray for her?" I spun around and saw the back of a wheelchair, and without thought or pause I put my hands gently on the shoulders of this woman and began to whisper a brief prayer. Suddenly, enormous power surged through her. Something really, really big had just happened: something vaster than could be seen or understood through the five senses. A gate had opened of divine relationship, set up by our mutual friend, God, the Holy Spirit. This was a bend in the road. If I could go back and paint a sign it would say, "You've just entered the God Zone! Unbuckle your seat belt. You are free to roam about the cabin. I'm in control and you are in for a ride!" Divine appointments are like that: exciting and a bit unpredictable.

Let's talk about courage. There are three categories: 1) extreme personal courage, beyond the boundaries, pushing the envelope; 2) sacrificial courage, laying your life down for somebody else; and 3) divine courage against all logic, reason, and even loving, good intention. Supernatural bravery is the stuff that got people named and recorded in the Bible. Kelly Tyler has, in my humble opinion, scored tens and zeros in all three categories. You can't really know ten unless you've really known zero: faced hopelessness, believed, and moved forward anyway. She and Ryan have believed God and personal prophetic promises followed by darkly disturbing pop-ups saying, "Impossible!" "Painful!" "Foolish!" and "Dangerous!" What they have believed is the voice of God, while being challenged by both the adversary of the soul, and their own human limitations. Hey, we check out of human limitations when we enter the God Zone!

It is with fear and honor that I introduce you to Kelly Tyler, a female "David" who rises from her wheelchair, steps on the neck of her "Goliath," severs his hideous head, and "walks it out" over his failed threats against her destiny. I'm so very proud of you, Kelly.

Mickey Robinson
Speaker, Author, and Friend

When It All Comes Down

> The LORD gave and the LORD hath taken
> away; blessed be the name of the LORD.
> Job 1: 21 (KJV21)

November 16, 1995 dawned as an ordinary day in Pelham Manor, New York. I strapped my toddler and six-year-old in the backseat of our car. Then I drove my husband to the train station where he would join hundreds of people like himself on the way to Grand Central Station, where he would then join thousands more on their way to work in the financial district of Manhattan. Then I, like thousands of other moms, drove back home to take care of the ordinary. The only difference was that this day the ordinary turned extraordinary and life as we had known it ended.

Shortly after we returned home, I began having sharp pains between my shoulder blades. I told my six-year-old, Joshua, that I was going to take a shower. I picked up my baby, Alexa, and put her in her crib for the last time. Ever. By the time I got out of the shower, I was blacking out. I got dressed with great difficulty and crashed onto my bed. I phoned a friend who said I should call 911. I did, but only to find out our town didn't yet have that service. I called the fire department, which in turn called an ambulance. I told Josh to get the baby and go next door. I didn't want him frightened by the ambulance. Finally, I called my husband, Ryan, and told him that I was going to the hospital, but added, "It's probably no big deal."

The firemen came, and I was able to stand up one last time but not able to walk. The firemen carried me downstairs where I was placed on a stretcher. Once inside the ambulance, my instinct was to fight with every prayer I could think up, but the Lord interrupted me with Zechariah 4:6: "Not by might, nor by power, but by my Spirit, says the Lord Almighty" (NIV). I wasn't sure why God had interrupted me, but I had the distinct feeling that he wasn't going to rescue me yet.

In the emergency room I was taken to triage. A doctor and nurse looked at me, stuck a much-too-large neck brace on me, and wheeled me into the main section of the ER near the nurse's station. I lay there ignored and becoming progressively more helpless. I tried in vain to move my body. I must have made some noise because a stranger asked if I was in pain. I said no, because I wasn't in pain. I couldn't feel much of anything.

I'll Do Anything If You Heal My Wife

Ryan found me in the ER, alone, on a gurney, paralyzed, and in near respiratory failure. "If this goes any further, I won't be able to breathe," I told him immediately. He tried to no avail to get a nurse to pay attention to me. "She's not going to stop breathing," she insisted without ever even looking at me. Thank God he jumped into action and took charge. He laid hands on me and commanded the paralysis to stop in the name of Jesus. Weeping, he cried out to God, "I'll do anything if you'll just heal my wife!" He then called my dear friend Lynne for prayer and to ask her to pick up our children. Afterwards, he called the only doctor we knew in the area, David Katz, who happened to be a pulmonary specialist. Dr. Katz in turn contacted a team of neurologists from Columbia Presbyterian Hospital in New York City.

Now the testing began. It was horrifying to see the doctors prick my body with needles and yet not feel a thing. Fear set in as the technicians asked me to move in different positions so they could get X-rays and I realized I was unable to move at all. I began singing worship songs in my head to calm myself down. Next, I was given a myelogram to determine if there were any breaks in my spine that the X-rays missed. The doctor inserted a long needle into my neck (one of the few places I still had feeling) and injected dye into my spine. It was so painful that all I could do was grit my teeth and pray through the whole procedure.

Afterwards, I was taken to the Intensive Care Unit. The doctors advised Ryan to stay with me through the night. They did not know what caused the paralysis or if the progression would continue. They only knew that if it did, I would go into respiratory and cardiac failure.

Between the Wings of the Cherubim

> There I will meet with you and, from above the mercy seat, from between the two cherubim that are upon the ark of the Testimony, I will speak intimately with you.
>
> Exodus 25:22 (AMP)

I awoke before dawn the next day to see Ryan standing at my bedside. "What are you doing here so early?" I asked.

"I never left you." His answer spoke volumes, as if it were a word from the Lord that surpassed time and space, speaking to the present situation, the past, and the future all at once.

I tried to understand why he stayed, but couldn't completely grasp the gravity of my situation. "I'll be right back," he promised with a kiss to my forehead.

And then I was alone, in the dark, with no sensation or movement except in my neck, head, and right arm. The nurse came in to take care of me. A sudden flash of panic rushed through me.

"Where's my arm?" I blurted out.

"It's right here," she reassured me as she moved my left arm so I could see it.

It takes time for the brain to adjust to an absence of sensation. I would repeatedly ask the whereabouts of my arm for several more days.

For the rest of the day, I teetered on the edge of consciousness. At some point I was aware that my husband and some other people were in the room. I could feel my awareness of the surroundings beginning to fade. I kept wishing I could tell someone to get my will, but I couldn't open my eyes or speak. I could feel consciousness slipping away more rapidly, and I thought if it did, I would never return to this realm. I knew I no longer had the strength to fight. Panic rushed over me in an unexpected wave as I thought of what my husband and children would do without me. Just as quickly, peace poured over me in a second wave, reassuring me that they would be fine. Yet, at the last moment, I cried out in my spirit, *But God, if I get a chance, I want to come back!*

Then there was nothing. No light. No sound. No feelings. No thoughts. Absolutely nothing.

I have no idea how much time passed, but suddenly, the silence broke. Someone was calling my name. It was as if I could feel myself being drawn back into this world. At first, my mind made no connection with the voice that seemed miles away. Suddenly, my brain made the connection. The voice belonged to Ryan. Instantly my emotions joined my spirit, which in turn engaged my will. I wanted not only to hear my husband's voice; I wanted to be with him. I fought with everything within me. It is the hardest fight I had ever fought. It took more energy than giving birth! I don't know how long I struggled, but I finally won. I became aware of where I was and that Ryan was right next to me, even though I was still only semi-conscious, unable to speak or open my eyes.

Ryan kept trying to get me to respond to my name. Finally, a nurse told him to ask me to move my finger if I could hear him. He obeyed, and so did I. As cheers and applause erupted, I thought the next thing I would hear was, "Houston, we have made contact."

Instead, a woman came to my bedside and explained that she needed to conduct a hearing test on me. I opened my eyes briefly. She placed earphones over my ears and instructed me to raise my finger every time I heard a tone. My hearing was fine. Next was the brainwave test. Several electrodes were placed on my forehead to monitor brain activity. I fell asleep until it was over. I awoke to Ryan announcing with relief, "Her brain is okay!"

I really wanted to answer him with, "Oh, when did that happen?" but I was still unable to speak.

I underwent tests the rest of the day. I had a full body cat scan, my blood was taken several times, and I was given high doses of steroids. I was attached to every kind of monitor imaginable as well as a catheter, since my bladder no longer functioned. Even still, I slept most of the day and through the night. I awoke the next morning before seven o'clock, completely alert, and buzzed the nurse. She appeared quickly and asked if I was okay. "Oh, yes," I answered cheerfully. "I just wondered if you could call my husband and have him bring my makeup bag up here." She was out of my room and on the phone before I could tell her that there was no need to rush or wake up Ryan. I still didn't get it. My frame of mind was so dramatically different than the day before that she wanted to let him know right away. He soon showed up in my room, makeup bag in hand as instructed.

Although I remained conscious, something felt very different. It was as if I had been turned inside-out. I could feel nothing in most of my physical body, but my spirit was intensely sensitive. I could tangibly feel people's prayers for me. They felt like thick, warm blankets swaddling me. I could also see people praying for me in different places. I saw a group of big men crying on their knees in prayer for me. Later, my brother, who is a minister, told me that he had been working with a particularly hardened group of ex-cons, but when he told them what had happened to me, they broke down and started crying and praying for me. I also saw my friend Sammy praying for me, as well as my grandmother. Later it intrigued me that both of them had gone home to be with the Lord several years earlier. I remember feeling intensely cared for, so much so that I commented to my husband as he tried to brush my tangled hair, "Ryan, I feel so loved!"

"You are so loved," he stated simply. Again, his words reached places inside my heart that seemed to have never grasped these words.

I remained "inside-out" the whole time I was in ICU. There really are no rooms in ICU. It's just one big ward with curtains separating the patients. One night a man was wheeled into the "room" next to mine. He voiced his displeasure and pain often and loudly. Every negative word pierced me, and when he used the Lord's name as a curse it seemed physically painful. He kept me up all night. Finally, I begged God to heal him so I could have some peace! When morning came I heard a nurse say to her co-worker, "That man is way too well to be in here if he can make that much noise!" He was moved to another ward within the hour.

The following night another man was brought into that room. He was so sweet and cried out for his wife often. My heart filled with compassion as I prayed for him through the night. His wife came the next day, and I asked the nurse to bring her to me. "Do you know her?" asked the nurse.

"No, but I'm about to," I answered. I just wanted to let her know how much her husband loved her and how much it meant to him that she was there and that I would continue to pray for him. She looked a little confused, but thanked me nonetheless.

In hopes of increasing my will to live, the doctors wanted my children with me as soon as possible. Josh was almost seven, and Alexa was just days away from her second birthday. Their first visit proved to be more frightening for them than reassuring. Alexa stayed huddled next to her daddy. Josh got into bed with me, but kept his eyes fixed on the heart monitor. I assured him that my heart was strong and that I was not in danger of dying. He relaxed only a little. That same night my heart rate dropped low enough to set off the monitor three times. After the third EKG the doctor looked rather concerned. "I'm not going to die," I promised. He didn't share my confidence.

After that my vital signs stabilized. More visitors came, and that did help my spirits. My dad and stepmom flew in, and my mother-in-law came and stayed for weeks to help Ryan and the kids. My dear friend from Texas, Herb Weinstein, somehow convinced the nurse to bring a phone in so he could talk to me. I still don't know how he did that, but it still makes me smile!

The Best Medicine

Sometimes a situation is so tragic and so humanly impossible to comprehend that it requires infusions of levity. One morning I convinced the nurse that I needed a tour of the ICU. There was this Pepto-Bismol-pink reclining chair on wheels left by the physical therapist. It wasn't really meant to be used as a wheelchair, but after sufficient begging I got my tour. I made it my mission to get a smile out of every patient as I waved to them from my pink "coach." My nurse thereby proclaimed me the "Queen of ICU."

Another time, one of my nurses was preparing a tub to wash my hair. "Oh no!" I declared in a tone of absolute seriousness, "Now we've really got a problem!"

She almost dropped the tub as she spun around and asked, "What's wrong?"

"I've got a zit right on my nose!"

"Don't do that to me!" she scolded. We both had a good laugh and joked that I was in the salon for a day of luxury. Sometimes the key to joy is knowing when not to take life on this earth too seriously, because nothing here compares to the realities in the spirit.

The physical reality of my situation hit me head on the day the therapists first tried to sit me up on the edge of my bed. Once they got me up, they let go of me for a couple of seconds. In that moment I realized that I couldn't even feel my feet touching the floor, but I could feel the dead weight of my utterly useless body as it fell forward into the arms of the physical therapist. I remember thinking, Okay, God. I get it. I am completely dependent on you! I only thought I got it. It would take a long time for me to grasp that concept.

Our former priest from All Angels Episcopal Church in Manhattan and friends Lynne and Char visited me the day I was released from the ICU and was placed in what they called the Progressive Care Unit, or PCU. Lynne came armed with one of her health food concoctions; however, I think her smile was more healing than the drink! The nurses got me ready and said goodbye. As I was being wheeled out, one of the doctors came over to wish me luck. "Don't worry about me," I grinned, "You're going to see me running in the New York City Marathon someday!" He was less than convinced.

Between the Wings of the Cherubim

The first part of what would prove to be a very long journey was ending. The past two weeks had been days that would change my life forever and would set me directly on the path that God had for me. It was during these first two weeks I spent in ICU that I had what would be the first of several heavenly visitations.

As I lay in the bed all alone I heard the Lord speak these words clearly, "between the wings of the cherubim." My heart leapt. As a teen I cried out to God often, telling Him how I longed to meet with Him, as Moses had, in the Holy of Holies. Now God Himself was echoing the cry of my heart. I looked to the right and saw two huge wings coming up over the side of my bed. I looked to my left, and there was an identical set of wings coming up over the other side of my bed. The two sets of wings met in the middle over my head, placing me in the center of His mercy seat.

Faith, Hope, and the Stuff of Earth

> Now faith is the substance of things hoped
> for and the evidence of things not seen.
> Hebrews 11:1 (KJV)

Sometimes the dichotomy between events on earth and what those same events represent in the spirit realm are so vast that it is difficult to reconcile the two. I had been praying for healing of scoliosis since I was eleven. God had spoken to me in 1991 saying, "I will heal you from the inside out." Just months before my paralysis, a man of God prophesied the same healing. While in my teens three different people in three different states told me that God would someday use me in the area of healing.

Just weeks before the paralysis struck, I cried out to God, reminding Him of these words and asking Him when they would come to pass. During that time I went to Newport, Rhode Island, and watched as the waves crashed against the craggy shore, sending ocean mist six feet into the air. The Lord spoke to me in the midst of that scene, simply stating, "Sometimes this is how healing comes."

At the time spoken, all of these words seemed straightforward enough, but in the stillness of paralysis they became enigmatic. As I lay in that bed, I felt the intensity of the warfare against my destiny and that of my family. Though I couldn't move my body, my spirit rose up inside me, and I spoke to the enemy of our souls as if we were face to face. When I get really mad, I speak my native tongue: Texan. I pointed my finger and spoke out loud, "Devil, you messed with the wrong girl this time. You're not going to win! I'm going to give more glory to God than ever before!" The battle was on!

For days my temperature spiked, and the nurses packed my upper body in ice to bring down the fever. I was miserable. At the same time, if the nurses tried to sit me up, I would pass out cold. My breathing was labored, and sometimes just talking was enough to cause me to lose my breath. All this resulted from the neurological damage that's origin still remained a mystery. It was so difficult and frustrating to breathe that at one point I cried out to God saying, "Lord, if breathing is going to be this hard, then make every breath worship to you!" From that moment on, when I struggled to breathe, I could feel His presence.

When they transported me from the PCU to physical therapy, I had to be wrapped in a sheet like a burrito and lifted by two people onto a gurney. During those sessions, I watched patients in their eighties run circles around me. The realization of how little I could do slowly began to sink in. The occupational therapist tried in vain to get me to move a joint in my finger. Nothing. Over and over again. Nothing. But what I could do was talk to her about the power of prayer and faith, and I did. Throughout those weeks in the PCU many of my doctors and nurses were Christians, and often I sensed they wanted to comfort me but were at a loss for words. I assured them that this was not as bad as it looked and that God was still who He said He was.

I found that though I could not lift a finger, I could still move the hand of God on behalf of others. Both of the roommates I had while in the PCU were elderly and dying. The first lady almost bled to death one evening during dinner. Though I was quite shaken by the incident, I was able to pray with her and comfort her many times. She recovered enough to go back to the nursing home. The next roommate was also near death. I ministered to her and her family as well and received a beautiful card from them upon her passing.

Honoring God was my weapon of choice in a war that had more fronts than my husband and I could possibly address each day. There were the obvious health concerns, our children to think about, mounting financial problems, legal issues, and yes, a marriage to somehow pay attention to.

Ryan continued working at Moody's Investor Services, while his mom helped at home. The local Italian Club paid for a nanny for the four months that I was hospitalized; a local lawyer offered his services pro-bono; the church brought meals; and my neighbors threw a party for Alexa's second birthday. God covered what we could not. One of my favorite adages proved true once again: "Life is hard, but God is good!"

Small Beginnings and a Promise

The church we had just started attending, St. Paul's Episcopal Church in Darien, Connecticut, sent two women to bring me communion. The Lord attended in a glorious way. The ladies left with such excitement that they told the priest, Carl, that he should visit me himself. He showed up in my room looking a little tentative. I smiled and said, "It may not look like much, but this is the beginning of my ministry." We were instant friends.

In the meantime the doctors struggled to find something that would explain why a healthy twenty-seven-year-old woman would suddenly become paralyzed. They tested me for everything from AIDS to Multiple Sclerosis. Finally, the only thing the neurologist could link to the illness was a tetanus shot I'd been given ten days prior to the onset of paralysis. I had actually argued with the doctor about getting the shot because I was not well at the time. He insisted. I gave in, and the rest, as they say, is history. The doctor who prescribed the tetanus shot was notified of the side effects but never contacted me. The neurologist contacted the insurance company with the diagnosis of an immunization side effect, but it was later changed to "transverse myelitis of an unknown origin." This means that the fatty tissue surrounding the nerves in the spinal cord have degenerated, but no one knows why. One of the hardest things to grasp was that once demyelization occurs, the results and the chances of recovery are the same as if the spinal cord is damaged in an accident

There I lay, too weak to chew my food or push the buttons on my hospital bed, struggling to breathe, and desperately trying to make sense of what God had said, when He dropped an even bigger spiritual bomb on me. I clearly "heard" these words in my heart, "You are going to have a son, and his name is Josiah." I was excited at first, and then I thought I'd lost my brain along with my body. I tried to reason it out. God had already promised my healing, so, I decided, He must be planning to give me a child afterwards. That sort of made sense, but I decided I better keep that promise to myself. The doctors already thought I was in denial because I insisted that I would walk again. I knew I needed a miracle. I also knew that miracles are no big deal for God.

The chasm between what the Lord was saying to me and what the doctors and my body were saying to me was too enormous to comprehend. Taking life one day at a time wasn't good enough anymore. This war required more than that. I had to take it minute by minute, thought by thought.

The Peter Predicament

I tell you the truth, when you were younger
you dressed yourself and went where you
wanted; but when you are old you will
stretch out your hands, and someone else
will dress you and lead you where you do
not want to go.

John 21:18 (NIV)

I had been through the valley of the shadow of death
and come out the other side with God's promises in
hand. I had seen angels, touched prayers, and glimpsed
part of the great crowd of witnesses that cheer us on. I
took all of this with me as the paramedics packed me
into an ambulance to be transported from the acute care

hospital to the rehabilitation hospital. "We're off to see the wizard and get you a new set of legs," the paramedic joked as he shut the ambulance doors, closing us in with the frigid December air. I hadn't seen the sky or felt fresh air in four weeks. I smiled at the paramedic and nodded my head, but I knew Park Rehabilitation Hospital was no Oz.

After we arrived at the rehab hospital, the paramedics wheeled me through the halls to my new room and placed me in a bed. I was met by the social worker on staff, Rose. We chatted and filled out forms. She asked a lot of questions then announced that I would probably be depressed within two weeks.

"Oh no, I won't!" I countered, "I've already got enough problems." I was indignant. Who was this stranger to tell me how I was going to feel and when? "Look," I said, "I'm sure I'm going to be sad, and I miss my children already; but depression is another story, and it's not going to be mine." Rose and I never exactly became friends.

I know exactly why people get depressed though. Right after Rose left my room, two nurses came in and without as much as an explanation, proceeded to take out my catheter and dress me in a giant diaper! This was not the fashion statement I was after. Next I was placed in a high-back wheelchair wearing only a hospital gown, wheeled into the hallway, and placed against the wall across from the nurse's station. Bewildered, I felt that I must have gotten lost in some obscure wing of hell! That, unfortunately, was just the beginning.

I arrived at Park Rehab on a Wednesday. In this particular wing of hell, Wednesday night is torture night, otherwise known as shower night. Because I was too weak to sit in a shower chair, I was stripped naked, placed on a gurney, covered with blankets, and taken to a shower room. It looked a little like a self-service car-wash with its gray walls and shower hoses attached to the wall. The attendant who showered me looked pre-pared to deal with toxic waste. She had a plastic shower cap on her head, rubber boots, rubber gloves, and a rub-ber overcoat. She stood back and sprayed me from a dis-tance, never speaking a word to me. It was humiliating and dehumanizing. When she finished, she covered me and took me back to my room. Even though blankets covered me, I felt totally exposed wheeling through the halls all wet.

Thankfully within a couple of weeks, I progressed to a shower chair. This method was far less humiliating but also more frightening because of my tendency to pass out. I still didn't have the ability to sit in that kind of chair, so I more or less slumped. The nurses were extremely patient and kind, which helped immensely. Whenever people asked how they could pray, I always asked them to pray on Wednesday because I was so afraid of showers. The Lord was gracious as always, and sent a new friend, Sally, who faithfully came every Wednesday night after my shower and always brought along her quick British wit and love for all things silly for our weekly "laugh-in."

There were others who came to pray as well. Alexa's Sunday school teacher was there one evening with Ryan and me. We were all praying, and the presence of God was particularly sweet. I started thinking of the prom-ise He'd given me in the hospital about a son named

Josiah. I didn't dare say a word about it, even though I really wanted to. There was a lull in the prayer, and Ellen spoke up. "I know this is going to sound crazy, but I think the Lord is saying that you're going to have more children." I laughed and cried at the same time. I relished the confirmation and the fact that I didn't have to try to explain it to Ryan.

Good Nurse, Bad Nurse

Life in a rehab hospital is a little like sleepover camp: lots of activities, little freedom, and bad food. I didn't exactly excel in therapy. My body just refused to cooperate. I slept sitting up my first day of therapy because I was so weak and exhausted. My physical therapist nicknamed me "The Weeble" because of my hopeless instability. I was told that I'd probably be dropped from rehab by the insurance company for failure to improve and placed in a nursing home. The thought terrified me. Ryan went to bat for me, and the insurance company agreed to let me stay three months. Although I was grateful to be able to stay, it proved to be one of the most difficult times in my life.

The lack of freedom took me totally by surprise. I was told when I could eat and sleep. The nurses woke me up several times a night to roll me over, and then I had to be up all day doing therapy. I never got enough rest. Once I asked my therapists to put me in bed during the lunch hour so I could at least rest a little before my afternoon therapy. When the nurse came in and found me, I was severely scolded and told never to do that again. I had no idea I was breaking a rule!

Sometimes the nurses made wrong decisions simply because they didn't understand the far-reaching effects of spinal cord injuries. Once I was explaining to a nurse how to get me out of bed without causing me to pass out. She was one of the good nurses who listened to her patients. She decided it would be best if there were two people to help me up. Her supervisor strongly disagreed, stating that I was lying and just wanted attention! My nurse then requested that her supervisor get me up herself since she didn't want to be responsible if anything should happen to me. The supervisor angrily agreed and came in and jerked me up by my one good arm, at which point I promptly passed out and she, I was told, started yelling for help.

Obviously, one of the hardest things was being separated from our children. Although I had done a little part-time work and finished my college degree since my children, Josh and Alexa, were born, I was almost always with them. I was there when they woke up, went to bed, got sick, and had bad dreams. No one else knew how to make Alexa's hair lay in ringlets or that Josh needed to cuddle after school in order to de-stress. Now I only saw them once a week and couldn't even hug them with two arms.

Josh visited me one day and, after he'd exhausted all the excitement he could get out of racing through the halls with me in my wheelchair, said with the depth and wisdom unique to a child, "Mom, remember playing basketball with me? Those are good memories, Mom."

We all had to live on those good memories and the grace of God for a long time.

Visitors in the Night

So am I made to possess months of vanity,
and wearisome nights are appointed to me.
Job 7:3 (KJV)

The days at Park Rehabilitation rolled along in a bearable fashion. Physical therapy remained difficult and discouraging. I was considered quadriplegic, even though I had some use of my right arm and hand. That didn't give me much to work with. I couldn't sit up or roll over or even lie on my stomach and prop myself up on my elbows. I even failed to progress at the tilt table. A tilt table looks like a medieval torture device. It's a flat table where the patient is strapped down and then gradually lifted up until he or she is in a standing position at a ninety-degree angle. The idea is to get the body readjusted to being in an upright position. To do so requires more blood pressure than lying down. I never got past forty degrees on that contraption except once when another poor patient across the room was accidentally dropped and my blood pressure went up!

I could use the triceps weight machine on both arms and the free weights with my right arm, but those were the only areas where I really made any progress. Occupational therapy was a lot more productive, mostly because my therapist, Kacey, understood how to connect with her patients and make just about anything seem funny. Relationships are everything to me, and therapy became better all around when I could connect with the therapist.

Rehab hospitals are full of characters, and everyone has a story. There was the twenty-one-year-old woman who had an aneurism and was left severely brain damaged. There was a guy next door to me and a woman around the corner, each paralyzed from Guillain-Barre syndrome, each with infant children.

There was another guy in his twenties recovering from a broken spine. He was temporarily in a wheelchair, and to force him to use his legs, the foot plate had been removed from his wheelchair. Basically, he had to putt around Fred Flintstone style, which was slow and tiring. He came up with a solution to his mobility dilemma and the other problem that plagued us both: boredom. He would pull up behind me and hook his feet under a bar on my electric wheelchair. I would put my chair into high speed, and we'd be off like a couple of kids playing in their neighborhood with go-carts. The only problem was that we were not in a neighborhood; we were in a hospital, and the nurses weren't always amused with our games. Some of them, however, enjoyed the comic relief.

Besides the occasional antics, places like rehab hospitals overflow with human suffering. The physical pain is "in your face" continually and the heartache palpable. Most of the patients were elderly, and many were confused and alone. It was an easy place to pray for people. Often if I was able to help another patient, that person's whole family would be touched. In one case, a sweet man we called Doc got confused and ended up in my room, thinking it was his own. When the nurse and I explained his mistake, he started to cry. I felt terrible for him, but I couldn't move or help him, so I told the nurse to hug him. She did, and then moved me close enough to hold his hand. That little act of mercy touched his family so much that they all became my friends. I was asked to pray for his daughter who was having a difficult pregnancy. The family called long after I left Park Rehab to announce the birth of their healthy grandson. This is why I say that when the going gets tough, the tough don't just get going; they give as they go.

My husband is one of those tough people. My paralysis had turned his world upside-down; but he kept going, and he kept giving. One day I wheeled into one of my therapy sessions, and Ryan was standing there. I was so surprised to see him that I didn't realize that it was him at first. When I finally recognized him, I was so touched that I cried. Later that morning I was trying to move my paralyzed left hand. "What do you want?" he asked when he saw that I was struggling.

"I just want to hold your hand," I answered. It was his turn to cry now.

He came every Friday after that to be with me during and after therapy, and he tried to come one other time during the week. These were precious times. They were times when we knew for sure that nothing mattered except that we were alive, together, and in love.

On Sundays he brought the kids to see me. They were such a gift! Alexa could always be heard talking to people in the hall. When asked what her name was, she could be heard proclaiming loudly and proudly, "Lubby!" as it was our habit to call her "Lovey." Just hearing my children's voices coming down the hall brought smiles that wouldn't quit. They showed up in my doorway one Sunday afternoon, and Alexa was wearing red-footed pajamas with a buttoned "trap door" on the behind, purple snow boots, and a winter coat. Her hair was... everywhere! I smiled at the sight and asked Ryan if they had gone to church.

"Yeah, why?" he asked innocently.

When I asked him about Alexa's pajamas, he looked a little confused and said, "Those are pajamas?"

Having family around was the best of times; being alone at night was the worst. My friend Lynne talked to me on the phone every night after visiting hours ended. I would have gone nuts or driven my husband nuts if she hadn't been there for me. I couldn't read very easily because holding books and turning pages was so awkward. Even talking was hard sometimes because of the difficulty I had breathing. Finally, after stringing together as many visits and phone conversations as I could, I had to face the darkness alone. Then my mind would race. Physically, it was very uncomfortable. I had to lie flat on my back until a nurse came to turn me (which was usually right after I fell asleep). Awake again, I worried about how I would ever get out in case of a fire. The hopelessness of my situation attempted to crowd out my faith. I would recount every miracle God had performed for me trying to fight off doubt, but sometimes that didn't even help.

The Visitation

One night was particularly horrible. My mind was under such a strong attack that I couldn't utter a prayer. Hopelessness and despair fell over me like a shroud. My spirit seemed as paralyzed as my body. At one point I felt the presence of evil, but I couldn't even fight. The evil presence seemed to mock me saying, "Your mistake was that you asked to live!" I couldn't find the energy to fight. I have never felt so helpless! I lay there tormented the entire night.

As soon as morning arrived, I called my friend Lynne for prayer. She is a trustworthy warrior with a lilting British accent and a beautiful countenance to match. She put the enemy in his place that morning, as she often does, and I finally had peace again. The Lord was making it very clear to me that following Him requires more than individual effort: it takes a team. I gained a new appreciation for the body of Christ that would only increase as I got more opportunities to see it in action.

I never had a night that rough again. In fact, after that experience, I had very special visitors in the night. Teresa was a dark Jamaican woman with a very polished accent and a million-dollar smile. She was the head nurse from 11:00 P.M. until 8:00 A.M. Teresa knew God, and together they turned the graveyard shift into a celebration of abundant life. She talked to me about Jesus and healing often, but she didn't stop there. She prayed every time she came, and when she prayed the power of God came! Sometimes the presence of God would come with such power that Teresa had to hold onto the bedrails in order to remain standing. It was so precious that I honestly thought she might be an angel. I always referred to her as "my angel in the night." One morning she came in to see me before she left work and gave me her home phone number. I smiled as I took the small piece of paper with the number written on it. "You know," I said, "I'm calling this number just to make sure you're not an angel." She laughed at the thought, but I was serious.

It was as if God was getting back at the enemy for harassing one of His kids. I never slept through an entire night, so when I woke up, I would talk to the Lord. On one occasion, I had my head turned to the left as I began talking to Him, I heard someone just behind my head say, "Why are you talking to the Lord with your head turned this way, when He's standing over there."

I turned my head to the right, and just as I'd been told, Jesus was standing next to my bed. I could only see Him from the neck down, but I was so happy He was there! His hands were resting on my bedrail. My mind suddenly flashed back to my childhood when my mom said prayers with me before bedtime. After prayer she always hugged me before she left, and then I always invited Jesus to come and hug me too. Lying in the hospital bed looking at Jesus, the first thing that came out of my mouth was, "Jesus, remember when I was a little girl and I used to always ask you to come and hug me?"

"Yes," He answered, "and every time, I came."

The next day was Saturday, and Ryan came to spend the day with me. About an hour into the visit I remembered what had happened the night before. I cried as I told him how the Lord had visited me. He took it in for a while, then asked, "Didn't you ask Him to heal you?"

"No," I answered, realizing that would have been the obvious thing to ask. "When I was with Him, I just forgot that I was sick."

Re-entry

He changes times and seasons.

Daniel 2:21 (NIV)

At times the situations we are in cause us to so long for change that we cannot foresee the challenges that change inevitably brings. It's like when a woman is pregnant; toward the end of the pregnancy she just wants the baby out of her body, into her arms, and to be on with her life. There is just one small problem. She will never get back to her life, at least not how she's lived it before the new baby. It's simply impossible. There is no going back. That is the definition of change.

The job of the staff at Park Rehabilitation Hospital had as its primary goal preparing me for just such a transition. Sometimes however, their way of going about it equaled the actual transition in awkwardness. While giving me breakfast one day, a nurse asked me if I wanted to talk about sexual matters. I nearly choked on my eggs! I told her I didn't and tried to be gracious, but she persisted. I assured her that if I had any questions, I'd speak to my family doctor. She wouldn't let up! Finally I burst into tears, so she dropped the subject. They sent another nurse to question me about a week later. This time I wasn't in shock. She told me that she had films on the subject. By now I was really getting offended! "Look," I said bluntly, "My husband and I didn't know what we were doing the first time around, and we figured it out. We'll figure it out again." With that remark, the nurse burst out laughing!

I also thought that would put a stop to the "sexual harassment," but no. There was more. Ryan came in for a discussion with the neurologist, and Rose sat in on the meeting as well. After the doctor left, Rose asked a few questions that I discreetly dealt with, and she left us to "think over" what she'd proposed.

"Do you have any idea what she just asked you?" I asked Ryan when she left.

"No," Ryan said, trying to figure out what he'd missed.

I had caught the inference because I had already been asked this question and thought that I had put the issue to rest.

"She just asked if you want a conjugal visit!"

"No, she did not!" he said in disbelief.

"I might have sex in some wild places, but Park Rehab is not going to be on my list!" I seethed.

I was really fed up! The paralysis had stripped me of every dignity imaginable, and now it felt as if the hospital staff was invading the intimacy of my marriage. Apparently they had concerns, but we did not. To be sure, we would be apart many months during my early recovery, but I knew that my husband was a man of honor. He honored my purity before we married, and I knew that he would honor our marriage now.

At one point in her well-meaning manner, Rose suggested divorce for financial reasons. The entire system was flawed and out of touch with the humanity they genuinely attempted to help. This is what happens when God and emotion are taken out of the equation. I felt more like a project than a person, reduced to a collection of scientific facts, and facts have no need for dignity and respect.

If you ever have the misfortune of being admitted to a rehabilitation hospital, there is something you need to know. They ask trick questions mixed in with all of the routine questions when someone first arrives. How was I to know? I assumed they were asking honest questions, so I gave honest answers. The question that really got me into trouble with Rose was this: "What are your goals when you leave Park Rehab?"

The question wasn't, "How much better do you think we, at Park Rehab, can make you?" Or "According to western allopathic medicine, how much recovery would be realistic to hope for in your situation?" Since the question was simply, "What are your goals for leaving Park Rehab?" My answer was simply, "My goal is to walk out of Park Rehab."

Poor Rose. Where I saw faith, she saw red flags.

She spent the whole time I was there trying to bring me into "reality." At one point she became so exasperated she decided she needed to bring in reinforcement. She called Ryan and told him that I was in denial. "She has faith," he said, knowing that she was fighting a losing battle. "What do you want me to do with her?" Realizing that she was on her own and that time was short, Rose redoubled her efforts. Her new crusade was to break me by making me realize that I was too sick to care for myself and to remind me daily that the insurance company would not cover custodial care. We had been through this argument before when the insurance company was threatening to put me in a nursing home but then relented and gave me three more months at Park. She felt more confident this time because she couldn't imagine the insurance company bending for me twice. I refused to give up, and Ryan prayed for God to make a way for me to have at least some custodial care. Rose looked at me one day and said point blank that it would never work. I looked back and said, "Never say never, Rose." I smiled, knowing she had just set herself up.

Just days before my release date Ryan called to let me know that although the insurance company would not budge, the company he worked for agreed to pay for me to have custodial care for six weeks. Between my mom, stepmom, and a friend from college, I was covered for another six weeks. Rose's response to my good news lacked enthusiasm. "Well, it must be really difficult to have to be taken care of by friends and family," she countered.

"I'd rather be taken care of by people who love me

than by total strangers," I said from experience. She left without saying anything more.

On the other extreme, was my occupational therapist, Kacey. We continued to have fun, and we shared a real bond. Kacey was an absolute Disney fanatic. She even spent her honeymoon there. She and her husband were planning another trip to the Magic Kingdom. Her vacation time was coming up around the same time I was to be released from the hospital, so she postponed her vacation in order to see me off. She had been a bright light in a dark place.

Going Home

The day of my release finally came on March 16, 1996, exactly four months after I had left my home in an ambulance. I sat dressed and ready for Ryan to come and take me home. Rose paid one last visit. She spoke more compassionately now. "I know you're not leaving here exactly how you'd hoped," she said. I had thought about that so many times and had time to examine it from every angle. I really believed that I would certainly have been healed by the time I left the hospital. After all, God had said that He would heal me. I didn't understand. All I knew was that God is who He says He is and that I had to hold on. All these months I had been stripped of everything: my freedom, my body, my family, and everything I loved on this earth, everything except my relationships with God and people. That's all that really matters anyway, so I decided that's not the worst position to be in. "Rose," I said, trying to speak in terms she'd understand, "It could be worse. I could have a guilty conscience, and that's a lot worse than being sick." With her job completed, Rose wished me luck and left me to await my departure.

Ryan came and got me and all my stuff into the car. I could see that snow still covered the grounds as we wound our way toward the large gated entrance. As we exited the gate, a tangible oppression lifted off me. I had been completely unaware of its presence until it left. Several of my friends later told me that they were quite aware of the oppression at the hospital. I was told that they felt it from the parking lot to my room, but once they got to my room there was peace. It was just one more confirmation for all of us that God was being faithful never to leave us nor forsake us.

I looked out the window, enjoying the sights of the outside world. Ryan asked if there was any place in particular that I wanted to go. "I want to see the water," I told him. We went to Long Island Sound, just a few minutes from our home. It comforted me to see the beach and playground that we had so often visited as a family.

We didn't talk. We were just trying to reconcile the life we'd known with the life we now lived. There was no reconciliation, only a mosaic of broken pieces that we hoped would somehow, someday make sense. We left the sound and drove on. I tried to figure out where we were but felt very disoriented. We turned down another unfamiliar street when I finally asked where we were going.

"Kelly," Ryan turned to me with a look of disbelief, "This is our street."

I looked again. It looked a little more familiar this

time. Then we got to our house. There was a newly built wooden ramp in front with little flowers painted on it. It was a gift from the local Junior League. Then, in the leaded window of this old house, I saw the first familiar sight: a little blond boy with the look of Christmas on his face shouting, "They're here!"

Josh ran out the door, greeted me, and eagerly waited as his dad took me out of the car and placed me in the wheelchair. Together they wheeled me into the house to greet Alexa and Ryan's mom. It was so good to see everyone and to be out of the hospital, but this house I'd lived in for seven months didn't even look familiar. "I like your house," I said looking at Ryan. "This is your house, too," he reminded me. I didn't care whose it was or where it was. It wasn't an institution, and I had my family.

My mom flew in from Texas later that day. It wasn't the appropriate time to cry, so we didn't. Later, I was placed on the couch in the family room. Alexa crawled up next to me with her pajamas and a diaper. Although both grandmas offered to help her, she refused and insisted, "Mommy do it!" I couldn't possibly tell her no, so after convincing the grandmas that we could do it, Alexa and I worked together and somehow managed to get her diapered, dressed, and ready for bed.

Then it was my turn. Ryan got me up our very steep flight of stairs via a chair climber. It was like an escalator, except it had a small seat to sit on and it went up the wall of the staircase on a track. It was the only way I could get up to my bedroom, but it wasn't a flawless method. First of all, going up and down often caused me to lose consciousness, and second, since I was unable to sit up, someone had to walk up or down in front of me to keep my upper body stable. Once I was at the top, Ryan carefully unbuckled the seatbelt while holding me up, then picked me up and placed me in a wheelchair. Then he wheeled me to my room, picked me up, and put me in my hospital bed. The process exhausted me. Next, I had to be undressed. Everything had to be done for me. Every zipper, button, and snap had to be fastened and unfastened for me. Getting shirts on and off was particularly difficult because my left arm, hand, and shoulder were both paralyzed and frozen. Moving them caused a great deal of pain. After all of that, Ryan had to help catheterize me, diaper me, and redress me.

So this was the change I had so longed for and the life I'd come home to. This life was as unrecognizable to me as my crippled little eighty-five-pound body and the street I lived on.

A Season of Questions

But where can wisdom be found? And
where is the place of understanding?

Job 28:12 (KJV)

The same hope that had given me the strength to
endure four months in the hospital left me feeling hol-
low, with more questions than answers now that I was
home. God had been so good and answered so many
prayers, but the one prayer we all wanted a yes for,
remained unanswered. At least I was home, though.
Ryan took two weeks off to help me settle in. It was not
exactly a vacation for him, but it was the sweetest gift
he could have given me. One morning he got me up
for a shower. My tiny frame was crumpled in a shower

chair, and I almost passed out in the few feet we traveled from the bed to the bathroom. Recognizing the situation, Ryan took my ankles and propped my legs up on the bathroom counter. As I became less dizzy, I looked up and caught a glimpse of myself in the mirror. It was a shocking image and hard to see. Just then Ryan looked down at me. "You're so beautiful," he said smiling. My eyes filled with tears as I wondered what he saw. He got me into the tub, held me up, and was bathing me as music played on the radio in the bedroom. The words of the song echoed a truth that settled in my heart. "I don't know much, but I know you love me, and maybe that is all I need to know." That was it. That's all I knew. I didn't know how I was going to be a wife or mom without use of my body. I didn't know why I wasn't healed or when I would be. All of the stuff I ever thought I knew about life and God made no sense now, but what I did know was that God loved me, my family loved me, and for the moment, that was all I needed to know.

On Monday the house was fully staffed. Ryan was home. My mom was there. The nanny was there, and the nurse's aide came. Ryan stayed to show the aide what I needed, but she didn't seem to appreciate his help. They got me up for a shower. He tried to explain how it best worked for me, but she insisted that she'd done this before and knew what was best. A few minutes later she dropped me on the shower floor! By the time I got picked up, cleaned up, and put back into bed, it was time for lunch. The aide brought my lunch and put it in front of me, but the trauma of the morning had shaken my last bit of strength; and I couldn't stop the tears from escaping my eyes. I sat there in my hospital bed as the tears defied my best efforts and landed in my lunch. "Crying isn't going to help anything," the aide scolded. I couldn't help it, and I couldn't stop it. I felt so helpless and humiliated as she scolded me like I was a spoiled child whining to get my way. Finally I told her that she could go and asked her to get my mom.

As soon as my mom hugged me, the floodgates opened and I sobbed. I was so discouraged and felt so miserable that I told my mom I wished God had let me go to heaven when I was so close. "I've already released you," she said. The reality of what we were saying suddenly hit me and I looked up at her smiling through the tears and hair hanging in my face, "He's not letting me go home, Mom." We hugged, and about that time we heard some loud conversation downstairs as Ryan apparently fired the aide and the nanny and sent them out the door. My mom and I looked at each other; she threw her hands in the air and exclaimed, "Praise the Lord!" Immediately the atmosphere in our house changed. Ryan walked upstairs half expecting us to be angry that we were without help, but was instead greeted with hugs and thanksgiving. He had overheard the nanny and the aide gossiping about me and my crying. That hadn't gone over very well with my protective husband. I was so thankful! The three of us prayed together and asked God to send us two new helpers of His choosing.

Within a couple of hours we got a phone call from a neighbor. She told us that she had a very good nanny but had to release her and wondered if we had a need for one. We met Sandra that afternoon, and she came to work the very next day. The next morning a new aide was sent out as well. I was terrified. I was completely helpless, and even though I had Ryan and my mom, I felt that I was totally at the mercy of this person. I heard the doorbell ring, and I could hear her coming up the stairs. I think I literally held my breath until a very dark face peered around the corner and into my room. "Hello," she said with a melodic Haitian accent, "My name Islande Israel." I breathed. She smiled. We had matching wide smiles with big white teeth. I knew I loved her already. I told her that I was afraid of the shower, so she bathed me in the bed, the whole time singing hymns over me. When she washed my face, she always called me her pretty, pretty baby. The love of God poured through this beautiful vessel. God had answered our prayers.

When it was time to get me up, Alexa appeared in my room and stood in front of Islande. With as much authority as she could muster in her two-year-old voice she said, "Don't drop my mommy!" We all assured her that Islande would be careful, but she stayed very near to make sure of it.

Over the next few weeks Islande and I got to know each other, sharing our faith and encouraging one another. We prayed every day and always invited Sandra to pray with us, which she graciously agreed to do. Sandra was Jamaican, and true to her nationality, she was very kind and laughed heartily. The children loved her. I was thankful to have her. During one of our early prayer times I asked Sandra if she'd ever given her life to Jesus. She told me no. I asked her if she'd like to. She told me no. So every day Islande and I included her in our prayer time, and every day I asked her if she was ready to give her life to Jesus. She always said no but always came back to pray with us.

Islande had the most incredible testimonies of miracles and God's faithfulness. She had something to encourage me with every day. Many times she told me, "God will heal you. I know this. I know these things." Then she would back it up with one of her many stories. One day when I was particularly discouraged, she repeated, "God will heal you. I know he will."

"But when," I cried out. "When?"

"Oh, but it is a surprise!" she said, holding her finger up as if warning me not to question God's timing. That would be a lesson I wouldn't learn easily.

My mom's two weeks were up, and sadly, she had to go back to Texas. My stepmom arrived for her two weeks just before Easter. Ryan's two weeks were up too. I cried the day he went back to work. I just couldn't bear the thought of doing this without him, but I knew I must. We were going into more debt every day.

It always seemed that just when I thought I couldn't bear another moment, God sent a miracle to carry me through. The day before Good Friday, Islande, Sandra, and I gathered in my room for prayer. I asked Sandra if she'd given her life to Jesus yet, and she said no one more time. This time I said, "Sandra, what are you waiting on?"

She answered, "I can't."

"Why?" I persisted.

"Because I have a baby," she answered quietly.

"What?" I had no idea what she was talking about.

"I have a baby," she continued, "and I'm not married to his father."

"Oh, Sandra!" I said almost laughing, "Jesus doesn't care about that right now. He just loves you and wants you to know Him. He just wants a relationship with you. Is that what you want?"

"Yes," she said with tears in her eyes.

So she prayed with me a prayer of repentance and gave her life to the Lord. The sick room became a sanctuary, and we were filled with the unique joy that accompanies new life.

The next day Islande and Sandra were off work, but Ryan was off work too, and so he was home. After he got me dressed, a group from church came to take us to a Good Friday healing service. It was in a huge auditorium in White Plains, New York. It actually snowed on us while we waited to get in. Once in, I was carried to the ground level and laid on a cot and covered with blankets. I must have been quite a sight! The worship was good, but I slept through almost everything. I got plenty of prayer, but no healing, not even a little. We went home tired and discouraged.

Easter morning was the worst. We thought that for sure by now God would have healed me. We had a really bad day. Friends came, but they were just as discouraged as we were! We all believed in this miracle and in the God who promised it, but where was it? I got so discouraged that I said to God, "Lord, it would be easier to just accept my condition and go on. It's so hard to keep believing when nothing is changing. Can't I just pretend that this is your will?"

The answer in my heart was immediate. "No," He said. "You're going to fight for this one."

I looked up and smiled. "I knew it!" Even as I said it, my heart felt a little more courage. I didn't doubt what God had promised; I was just getting worn out with the battle. In that moment I understood just a little that this whole thing was more than about me. I prayed, "God, if I'm going to have to wait for my miracle, then I'm asking for you to allow me to pray for others and see them get theirs right away."

Sandra and I were on our own after the first couple of months. We couldn't really afford her, but the kids and I couldn't be left alone either, so we cut her days to Monday through Thursday. On Fridays I was alone in the mornings, the kids were in school, and at noon, when Alexa came home, a lovely retired couple from our church came to take care of us. What a blessing!

The mornings were a little rough for me sometimes. Once Ryan gave me some nuts before he left for work. I choked on one as he was running down the stairs. He ran back up, pounded my back until I coughed it up, and shouted as he ran down again, "No eating until I get home!" I guess he figured that I was less likely to die from starvation than choking, but it wasn't the solution I was looking for.

Ryan took me out to lunch for our first date since the paralysis. We went to this little bistro in a renovated cottage. The place was charming, and the food was great. Since I did not have enough torso strength to sit up, breathe, and eat at the same time, I had to lay my head on the table so I could chew my food. We knew it would take a long time so we brought our Bible to read. Ryan would feed me a bite, and I would take my time chewing; meanwhile he'd read to me. We were enjoying each other's company so much that it wasn't until we were leaving that we realized no one else was in the restaurant. The staff had been watching us for a while. They must have wondered about us. Maybe signs and wonders aren't always what we expect them to be.

The kids and I learned new ways to play together, too. In the backyard I would chase them around in my electric wheelchair with the water hose. I was surprised at how much fun they had. Alexa made tea parties on a regular basis and brought them to me in bed. Josh and Alexa had become extremely close while I was away. It was very sweet to see them. Josh was really good with Alexa when Ryan wasn't home. He would get her in and out of her crib and often changed her diaper. One day he got her from the crib and yelled, "Mom, she really stinks. I can't change her."

"Okay," I yelled back, trying to think of a solution. "Just bring her here," I directed, still not sure of what I was going to do. Josh obediently delivered the very smelly toddler to my hospital bed. I considered the situation and came up with a plan.

"Josh, you unzip her pajamas and take her feet out. If you hold her ankles, I can clean her." And so, with Alexa's cooperation and my one arm, Josh and I tackled the problem. This is how we learned to live. We faced one difficult, if not impossible, situation after another and learned that just about anything could be conquered with enough faith, creativity, and teamwork.

Dreams and Visions

Sometimes though, that still wasn't enough to ward off discouragement, frustration, and sheer exhaustion. I woke up one night with negative thoughts bombarding me. I refused to listen and prayed for sleep. As soon as I fell asleep, I was in a dream. I was in a church service and went to the altar for prayer. I walked up to a large man in a white suit with dark curly hair past his shoulders. I proceeded to tell him how desperately I needed healing as I rattled off all my symptoms. When I stopped to take a breath, he threw his head back and laughed out loud. He then looked me square in the eye and said, "Oh, you just need to believe!" I immediately woke up.

At first I was excited about the dream, and then I remembered it was Friday. I had physical therapy every Monday, Wednesday, and Friday back at Park Rehab as an outpatient. I hated it. I hated being in an atmosphere that considered hope false. I hated being around people who honestly believed that they knew better than anyone else how "handicapped people" need to live. If being there was dreadful, getting there was an absolute nightmare. First there was the whole process of getting bathed and dressed. Then I would be lifted out of bed and taken down the stairs via the chair climber. Often I would pass out on the way and be given smelling salts at the bottom to revive me just in time to be put on the bus. Then the fun really began. There were no belts to strap in my torso, so with every bump and turn my body jolted around like a little rag doll. Left turns were the worst because my body would be sent to the right, often banging my head against the bus window. I often cried quietly on these rides, hoping no one would notice. This was one of those days. I cried out to God to give me something to hold onto. I thanked God for the dream He'd given me the night before and apologized for needing more but asked for more anyway.

At that moment I sensed the Lord's nearness as I seldom had before. "You're here!" I exclaimed in my spirit. His smiling presence penetrated every layer of my broken heart. Nothing in my circumstances was different, yet nothing was the same. Everything changes when Jesus shows up. He was so real and approachable in those moments. He filled me with a joy that did not belong there.

I don't even remember what happened in therapy that day, but since it was Friday, Ryan came to pick me up. "Guess who showed up on my bus today?" I asked. He wept as I told him the story. I treasured those moments and was so impressed with the humanness of Jesus. He was so real and so easy to relate to. I never understood until then how very much like us God had to become to rescue us from sin and sickness and all the plans of the enemy. I never really understood until then to what great lengths He would go just to meet us where we are.

My next encounter with the Lord would not be so down to earth. It happened in the night while I was sleeping. I found myself in a strange place, surrounded by strange creatures. The creatures each had four faces, and I was terrified. Suddenly, I remembered the book of Ezekiel. Just as I realized that this frightening place was the throne room of God, I noticed that the creatures were now bowed down with their faces to the ground and I was the only one still standing. I dropped to the ground facedown as fast as I could. When I opened my eyes, I was at the feet of Jesus. I closed my eyes as He began speaking. I don't remember most of what was said, but I'll never forget how it sounded: like rolling thunder echoing in a great hall. His final words were, "Tell the people that I'm coming back soon."

Then it ended, and I was back in my paralyzed body, in my hospital bed on Washington Avenue in my own home. I was in awe and a bit confused. There was so much that I didn't understand. How could I be in His presence and not be healed? What was He doing in all of this? It was obviously much bigger than I could comprehend. Though I was thankful for these experiences, I didn't know how to live in this place between the realms. I just knew that I trusted Him.

Interconnections

So we, numerous as we are, are one body
in Christ (the Messiah) and individually we
are parts one of another [mutually dependent on one another].

Romans 12:5 (AMP)

Extreme and unusual experiences were beginning to
be more the rule than the exception. The people we
crossed paths with were just as diverse as the experiences themselves. Sometimes God brings people into
our lives for only a season, but it's at a crucial time that
helps pivot us into a broader dimension of our destinies.
Jay did just that. We met him or rather he followed us
to our car and insisted we meet him the Sunday before

I was paralyzed. It's as if he already knew he was on a mission.

As soon as he heard that I was paralyzed, he was all over it. He was the one guy who had absolute faith in my healing and also had the time to follow up and hang out with Ryan and me. We very fondly refer to him as our "crazy friend Jay." He is all energy and passion. His life's calling is helping people learn how to live natural, healthy, joyful lives. He actually had my husband convinced that raw corn is a perfectly good meal for small children and adults alike. I'm certain we were the only people in the state of New York with corn juice on the inside of our car's windshield. Ryan and Jay spent hours walking in the woods and praying together. Theirs were no girly-man, milquetoast, if, maybe, or please kind of prayers. Oh no, these were testosterone and Holy Spirit-energized, take-no-prisoners, it-must-be-as-God-has-spoken-it, storming-the-gates-of-heaven kinds of prayers. Being invited to one of their prayer meetings was like sitting ringside at an extreme boxing event. It was loud, exciting, and constant motion. There was even the real danger of being hit by flying saliva. The room sparked with faith and hope. I wondered what would happen in a church where men felt the freedom to express themselves to God like this on a continual basis.

The differences between the warmth of home and the sterility of Park Rehab were enormous and becoming too much for me to withstand. This is how God works at times. Things will be going along, and then the grace is gradually lifted until it's so unbearable that a change has to be made. I woke up on a day that I was supposed to go back to Park. The dread of going overwhelmed me, but I didn't say a word. Then Ryan pulled one of his I-can-feel-your-thoughts moments. "What's wrong?" he asked.

"I don't want to go back to rehab," I said, about to cry.

"Then don't," he said.

"Really?" I couldn't believe it. I so wanted to stay home. After all, the Park therapists gave me no real hope anyway, but I still had the residuals of an institutionalized mindset that made me afraid to actually leave formal rehabilitation. I don't know what I thought they could do to me, but in some strange way I felt they would be angry with me. When one has been at the mercy of others who control every aspect of your physical life, a great deal of fear comes in, and autonomy goes out.

That was a great day. The decision to stop therapy was so liberating. I took part of my life back that day. Sandra even seemed to feel the change in the atmosphere. With my new found freedom, I decided to visit a friend who lived a couple of blocks away. We used to meet on her patio for tea when I was well. Karin is a wonderfully compassionate and intelligent woman with a robust Austrian accent. She is one of those people that I knew I would be friends with the moment I met her. Even though we had just met three months before I was paralyzed, Karin visited me in the hospital and even collected money for me at the crosswalk to the school our children attended. I couldn't wait to surprise her with a visit. Sandra got me up, ready, and out the door. I told her I'd be back later and was off down the street in my electric wheelchair. Sandra's boyfriend was working on a house across from Karin's. I waved to him as I whizzed by and laughed to myself as he stared at me with his mouth open before I crossed the street. Arriving at my destination, Karin greeted me with a hug and of course, followed it with a great cup of tea.

Among Strangers and Friends

After that little adventure, I was ready for something more. I had to get healthier. Jay had talked a lot about fasting for health purposes, and since Ryan had fasted with some significant results, we contacted an expert in therapeutic fasting. His health institute was providentially located just thirty minutes from Ryan's family in Ohio. We decided to do it, knowing, of course, that it was not some miracle cure, but understanding that my body needed a chance to detoxify and rest. Our church graciously provided the money necessary to make this happen. The only bad part was that I would have to give up my family again because the treatments usually took at least three weeks. We decided to let Josh stay with his grandparents as long as I was at the institute because I thought I would get to see him more that way. Alexa stayed with Ryan because we didn't want to lose Sandra.

I cried as Ryan drove me from his parents' home to the institute. Leaving my kids when we'd finally been reunited after my hospital stays was excruciating. Then I had this thought, At least Josiah is with me. It wasn't in some spooky spiritual way that I felt he was with me but in the sense that any promise that God gives, once we've received it by faith, becomes a part of us. It's like being pregnant in the spirit. The old timers referred to it as a "burden from the Lord." It's the revelation that the promise God has given is real in the realm of the spirit and that God wants it prayed into the natural realm. Off I went with my two spiritual seeds (the healing and Josiah) into more uncharted territory.

We pulled into the driveway of what would become my home for the next three months. It was an old wood-framed farmhouse with a big front porch. We were greeted by two Amish women in bonnets and long dresses. These would be my new caregivers. I was taken from the car and shown to my new room where I was placed in a twin-sized bed. There was a large mural of a pastoral scene on the wall in front of me and a window next to my bed, which looked out onto the front lawn.

Next I met the doctor. He was a slight, matter of fact man who, I would come to realize, never wore any color except brown and tan. Although he was small of stature and in his seventies, he was strong enough to pick me up to weigh me. He took my blood and my vitals, and then he was off. Ryan stayed for dinner, and then after that, I was on my own again.

There were patients from all over the country as well as Mexico, Canada, and Europe. The people there had many different ailments from Crohn's disease to failing eyesight. Some were just there for general health maintenance. Most of them would be doing forty-day fasts. I mean real fasts, with zero food and only water to drink. We weren't even allowed to use toothpaste. The length of the fast always depended on the results of the patient's blood work. The plan was for me to fast as long as my tests showed it was beneficial.

My fast began immediately. I was told that after the first week or so the hunger would subside. It never did. I had a roommate for a while, and we talked about food most of the time. The days were long and sometimes lonely, but I was able to talk on the phone and meet some interesting people. One day an older man, who was also fasting, came in to meet me. He said his name was Dallas Frazier. He had an easy southern drawl which I appreciated and missed. I told him I was from Texas and asked him why he was fasting. He told me he was seeking God. Now it was getting interesting. We talked about the Lord awhile, and then I asked him what he did for a living. "I'm a minister now," he said, "but most of my life I've been a song writer."

"Cool," I said, "I like to write too, but not songs. What kind of music did you write?"

"Mostly country," he answered nonchalantly.

"Wow. What did you write?"

"I wrote a song called "Elvira," he said without excitement.

"Oh yeah. I remember that song," I replied.

Actually, that song was a hit before I was born, and what I remembered was the second time it was later released by The Oakridge Boys. In fact, I had no idea I was talking to a legend in country music. His songs were sung by everyone from Elvis Presley to George Strait, and he'd earned just about every award available, not to mention that he was inducted into the Country Music Hall of Fame. I didn't know any of that, and he never told me. I had to look it up myself.

In fact, when I asked if he wrote anything else, he said, "I don't talk about it much. That was before I knew Jesus." Instead, we talked about whom we both love most. I was touched by his heart for God. He was real. He had tasted and seen what the world had to offer and was sick of it. He had tasted and seen that the Lord is good, and that's all he wanted. We were writers on the same page.

I had plenty of time to seek God while I was there. The first subject I tackled was a nagging question, really a taunt of the enemy, which went like this, "What makes you so sure that out of all the people who have prayed for healing, you're going to be healed?" While fasting, I became strong enough to bear weight on my left arm, so reading was much easier now. Although I had been raised knowing what the Bible says about healing, I searched out every Scripture on the subject just in case I'd missed something. I found none to support doubt or giving up, so for me, that was settled.

My next subject was Josiah. The Lord had given me the promise and even his first name, so now I asked God to give me his middle name. As I was praying, the Lord took me to this Scripture: "For the kingdom of God suffereth violence and the violent take it by force" (Matthew 11:12, KJV).

Wow! I thought, *A prayer warrior; but I asked for his name, Lord.* I couldn't figure it out, but I started sharing the Scripture with those who knew about Josiah. The funny thing was that every time I tried to tell someone, I misquoted the Scripture and said, "The violent take it by storm." After about the third time, I thought, That's it! His middle name is Storm! So that was settled now too. The baby God promised me was named Josiah Storm Tyler. I liked it.

The Lord continued to reveal to me the wonder of His true Church, the body of Christ, and how awesome it is when it is operating in the way He intended. I was slowly growing to appreciate the beauty of His Bride through the many true believers He sent my way.

Living a summer with two Amish women was an opportunity to experience a part of the body that I knew little about. Wilma was intelligent, strong, and capable. She ran the place and prepared all the food and fresh fruit and vegetable drinks. She had a great sense of humor. Erma assisted Wilma and was compassionate with a childlike desire to please. I was a lot of extra work for them, but they served me without resentment. They were both fun to be with. Their lifestyle based on simplicity and community was refreshing in a culture that rewards us for how many things we can check off our To Do List and leaves little time to really be a part of the people's lives around us. It's funny because Wilma, Erma, and I were all out of our elements. We had all been in different ways taken out of our cultures, and stripped of them, we had all that mattered in common.

The fast only lasted two weeks because that's all my body could handle at the time. Wilma came with my first meal the next day, half an avocado. She fed it to me as I was too weak at first. I've loved avocado ever since! Ryan and the kids came to visit. I hadn't been able to see Josh as often as I had hoped, even though he was only half an hour away. Although I was terribly homesick, we decided that since I was already there, I would fast again and get as much out of this as I could.

More Changes Ahead

Even though I lay in the bed all summer seemingly doing nothing, there was a lot going on. God was busy making more connections that would position us for the next strategic move He had for us. I stayed in touch with our church: St. Paul's Episcopal in Darien, Connecticut. One afternoon as I spoke with our priest, Carl, we realized that his wife, Greta, was at a conference near me in Ohio. I was staying near the airport, so Greta and her friend were able to visit me on their way back home. It was great to see some familiar faces but even better to hear about what God had done in the meetings they'd attended. They had been at St. Luke's Episcopal Church in Bath, Ohio. Greta told me she'd asked that my name be put on the church's prayer list and gave me the church phone number in case I wanted to go to a healing service. I thought that was great but had no idea that I had just been introduced to the next part of my destiny.

Sometime in the following days, the Lord revealed to Ryan and me separately that we were to move to Ohio. Soon after that he came to Cleveland for an interview and got a job at an investment bank. The following Saturday evening, he came to take me to a healing service at St. Luke's. I weighed all of seventy-five pounds at this point and hadn't sat up all summer. When he put me in the car, I immediately noticed a difference in my ability to sit. According to blood tests, my liver was healthier, and I no longer had to be catheterized. This was more progress than I had made in the hospital, but it didn't change my life much. I was still unable to sit without support. My left arm was useless, and my left hand still a gnarled little claw.

We traveled the hilly road to the little blue clapboard church. It was a lovely drive, and I was excited to be in a church again. Ryan got me out of the car and into my chair. We got up to the door where someone helped us in. The second the door opened, a wind blew on us, and I immediately recognized the presence of the Holy Spirit. I looked up at Ryan, "Did you feel that?"

"Yes," he whispered.

We went into the service and enjoyed worshipping and basking in the love of the Lord. Then it was time for prayer. Nothing we'd ever experienced was quite like this prayer service. Some people sat quietly. Others lay prostrate, and still others groaned in intercession. Someone laid hands on me and prayed for healing, and the priest just came by periodically and touched me and said, "More, Lord." I thought it all rather strange, but I liked it. When we got back in the car, I asked Ryan what he thought.

"I don't know," he answered honestly, "but God was there."

That seemed to be the lesson of the hour. We were learning to know God and His character and His presence no matter how far out of our comfort zone He took us. God is God outside of our human understanding and theologies. He is God when we approve of His ways and when we don't. God is God. He is holy and just and always good. He is. And that never changes. Everything else is up for grabs.

With the fasting completed, we gathered our things, boarded a plane, and went back to New York to prepare to move. It had been an adventure that led to the next piece of God's plan, all because the body of Christ was working together.

Separation Anxiety

I pray that now at last by God's will the way
may be opened for me to come to you.
Romans 1:10 (NIV)

Living a life committed to obeying the will of God is definitely a walk of faith. We have no human way to know what lies ahead, aside from the excerpts the Lord shares with us. That leaves a lot of room for the unexpected, and it gives us plenty of opportunities to wholly trust the Lord. The incredible feeling of having our family together again and the hope of living together in Ohio was fleeting. It was already August, and Ryan needed to start his new job in September. It became apparent that our house would not sell in that short amount of time, and we could not afford payments on another residence. Also, Josh needed to begin school, so his grandmother came to take him back to Ohio and get him enrolled. Because of the situation, we decided to ask Ryan's parents if we could stay with them until our house sold.

My mother-in-law broke the news to me that I couldn't live at their home since they had no downstairs bedrooms. She told me to make arrangements to stay with my family in Texas. I agreed, but I would not go without Alexa. We had been apart for a total of seven months, and I couldn't bear to leave this little two-year-old without her mother again. Just a year before it would have been unthinkable that someone other than Ryan or me would decide where we or our children would live. We as adults think we are entitled to make our own decisions, but often the Lord allows situations that remind us there is actually very little that we control.

Josh left our house the next day literally kicking and screaming. I was heartbroken, and Ryan felt that his hands were tied. I did not qualify for any public assistance because I was married. Again a social worker pointed out that divorce would allow me to receive assistance and I could still live with my family. Even if that had helped us stay together, for us, divorce was not an option.

My mom and dad both lived in Texas, and since my mother felt ill equipped to care for me on her own, my dad and stepmom took Alexa and me in. There was no doubt that whoever ended up with us would have to make sacrifices, and for those sacrifices made, I am grateful. My stepmom and her mother are both kind and compassionate and did their best to make feel as comfortable as possible. Alexa went to a preschool, and I went back into a rehabilitation program. The therapist was the worst I would ever experience. He actually called me an idiot for not being capable of performing an exercise to his liking. Years later Josh told us that he woke up depressed every day as he started third grade in Ohio with only half his family. As for Ryan, he struggled to adjust to a new job and new city without his best friend and little girl. My dad's phone bill increased the longer we stayed, reflecting our growing discontent. Once again, just as the grace seemed to be running out, the Lord found a way to fill us.

Divine Appointments

Somehow I found out about a conference at St. Luke's, the church in Ohio. I called Ryan and told him that I wanted to go. Without hesitation, he bought Alexa and me airline tickets. He and his mom found a nurse to care for me while I was there, and Ryan just carried me up and down the stairs since there was no downstairs bedroom. Alexa and I arrived on a Friday. She awoke Saturday morning screaming with an earache. Thankfully, Ryan had already found a good doctor who was kind enough to treat her on a Saturday morning. Afterwards, Alexa fell asleep for four hours and never had another problem. The Lord had provided again.

That night we made our way to the church. Because it was a conference weekend, we really didn't know what to expect. The place was packed. The sanctuary was full and so was the foyer. I didn't know who was ministering and couldn't see him either. His words were filled with power, and the congregation was fully engaged. I was thrilled to be there and to know God was present. I remember thinking, This is what I've been waiting for. I had longed to witness the power of God that up to then I'd only heard about. After the service there was a time for prayer. There was no way to get me and the wheelchair to the front, so I just sat taking in God's presence that permeated the atmosphere. Eventually a lady came and prayed for me. She asked if I wanted Mickey to pray for me as well. "Who's Mickey?" I asked.

"He's the man you heard speaking, Mickey Robinson."

"Oh," I said. "Well sure, if he wants to."

The lady disappeared into the crowd. I was worshipping with my eyes closed when she returned with Mickey.

He stood behind me with his hands on my shoulders as he began to pray. The power of God flowed through him so intensely that my body went forward, my head touching my knees, and a sound impossible for me to make with my weak lungs, bellowed out of my mouth. That shout still comes on me in rare occasions of deep intercession. Next, I sat straight up from that bowed position, something still impossible as I write. God's presence was so strong that we were all surprised that I didn't get up right then!

After praying for me, Mickey came around and knelt in front of me. I saw his face for the first time: terribly scarred from burns on one side and perfectly normal on the other. His face so well reflects who he is:

a man who has deeply suffered on the one hand, and on the other, a man who exhibits the true wholeness that only Christ can give. In that way, he is a visual representation of the whole body of Christ, wounded and redeemed all at the same time.

That night he didn't tell me his own story of tragedy and survival (and he has an amazing one), but he told me one that was even dearer to his heart, the testimony of his first son, Michael. Michael was twenty-one, had suffered from cerebral palsy since birth, and had been in a wheelchair his entire life. As his dad, Mickey has probably suffered more loving and hurting for Michael than he has from his own injuries, and in that suffering, God has created deep wells of love and compassion for others suffering similarly. I drank deeply at those wells that night and have many times since. As Mickey and others like him have loved and encouraged me, I've learned to value suffering and allow God to create in me those same kinds of wells.

After Mickey left the crowd started to thin, so Ryan took me into the sanctuary. A man with a little boy approached us and asked if they could pray for me. The man, who is now our dear friend Dr. John Wagler, may have prayed over me. I don't remember. What I remember is his little boy, about the same age as Josh, praying over me with such authority and speaking into my life such discernment that all I could do was cry.

We took the whole family back to church the next day. Then it was time for Alexa and me to leave again. The weekend had been everything I'd hoped it would be and more. It was so good to be able to see and hug

Josh and Ryan. To add to the blessing, God had met me personally in an incredible way.

It was increasingly more difficult to separate our family each time we had to do it. I went back to Texas with a new determination to find a way for us to be together. Our house in New York still hadn't sold, so that obstacle still remained. The other huge obstacle was the amount of care I required on a daily basis. The costs of having someone stay with me during the day to look after me and help with meals was simply too much for us. I contacted every organization I could think of that offered help to handicapped people but always came up short because I was married and my husband made too much money for me to qualify. Again and again I got the same answer: if I were divorced or single I could live anywhere or with anyone, including my husband, and still qualify for help. I was exasperated and feeling hopeless. I started thinking about Mickey Robinson and wondered if he had any ideas. Feeling more than a little awkward, I phoned St. Luke's office and asked how I could reach Mickey. The receptionist asked for my name then exclaimed, "You're not going to believe this, but Mickey just called here asking how to get in touch with you!"

So I wasn't nuts! I felt relieved. I immediately called Mickey, and we talked for a very long time. He was in the same predicament trying to find care for Michael. He had no answers either, but I felt comforted by the mere fact that someone cared and understood.

Reunion

Alexa's third birthday came and went, and Ryan and Josh came out to Texas to be with us for Thanksgiving. After that, the grace ran out. There was no sign of the house selling, but no matter what, we knew we had to get our family back together. Plans fell into place for us all to live with Ryan's parents, and Alexa and I were in Ohio two weeks later for Josh's eighth birthday. His mom had helped find someone to care for me part time, and though I did have to stay upstairs until Ryan got home every day, it was still better than being apart.

Ryan's mom had planned a great party for Josh. When it was over, I told him how happy I was to be with him on his birthday. He responded with, "When are you going back to Texas, Mom?"

"I'm not," I answered.

"You mean you're staying until Christmas?"

"No. I mean Alexa and I are moving here to live."

He didn't answer. He just looked at me for a moment and then pounced on me with a big hug!

Living in Texas had become so depressing for me that I had begun to wonder if I'd ever be happy and have fun again. The first weekend back with my family was incredible. Ryan got me dressed, gathered the kids, put us all in the car, and we were off to the mall to Christmas shop. I'll never forget the feeling in that car. It was better than Christmas morning. We were all so full of joy and contentment just because we were together. If only I could bottle that thankfulness for all the times we get on each others' nerves!

Three months later we got the good news that our house in New York had sold. We were blessed to find a great rental home near Ryan's parents in a market that did not lend itself to rental properties. It was so good to feel like a family again in our own space. The kids loved the yard and the creek in the back. Josh's school bus stopped right outside our house, and Ryan's mom took Alexa to preschool three times a week. Ryan's hours were really long, but we were used to that; and we finally started the long process of trying to get our lives back together.

It was incredibly difficult. Creditors called during the day, and the enormity of the changes we were all going through haunted us at night. We were both sick of the fact that Ryan had to do everything for me. My mom heard of a doctor near her home in Texas who had great success with difficult cases like mine. I spoke with him on the phone and really liked him. After considerable prayer, we decided that I should go back to Texas for around a month.

Just before I was scheduled to leave for Texas, I got a call from Gretsie, our pastor's wife, who was organizing a women's conference in our church. She really wanted me to attend, but I had to decline. Ryan would have to come along to take care of me, and I would have to get someone for the kids. It all seemed like too much trouble. Nevertheless, Gretsie wouldn't let the so-called obstacles stand in the way. She found Kathie, another lady in the church and a former nurse, who said she would be glad to take care of me and even cover my expenses. How could I say no to such kindness? I definitely knew God was calling me to go, otherwise I would never have agreed to allow a total stranger to dress me, clean me, and sleep with me for two days. No way!

The conference was good and the worship incredible. Little did I know that the Lord would use that weekend to change my life. As I got to know Kathie, I started sharing with her some of the things on my heart. I had shared these things with others before, but when Kathie heard them she knew exactly how to help me. I had some really strong generational strongholds that had to be broken, and I was so glad to finally meet someone who not only understood but could connect me with people who were skilled and anointed to pray for me. I really wanted to get prayer before I went to Texas, and she helped get it organized. In my own prayer and preparation for this very important time, the Lord brought to mind several key people and events. One of those people was a cousin that I'd lost contact with. I called my mom to see if she knew how I could contact her, but she had lost touch with her as well.

The prayer time finally arrived, and I was filled with anticipation. I really had no idea what to expect, but I knew that God was going to meet me and I'd waited a long time for this. Kathie picked me up, and I talked the whole way there. I even told her how God kept putting this particular relative on my heart. We got to the church and went right to work. It was the most peaceful, holy prayer time I'd ever been in. After the prayer the woman leading it asked God to do something for me in the next two days to confirm what He'd accomplished.

The very next day I got a call "out of the blue" from the cousin I couldn't locate! She would become a vital part of my inner healing over the next several years of my journey. God's timing was impeccable, as always.

Two days later I left for Texas to begin the treatments. This trip to Texas was less stressful than the last. I went of my own volition and with the hope of seeing more healing. Both children were with me, and Ryan made plans to visit every other weekend. He still wasn't sure where we should put down roots, and true to His character, God had more planned than we could imagine.

My doctor was a Christian, and his staff prayed for me every day. He discovered that I had heavy metal poisoning from a combination of sources. He gave me medicine to draw the metal out of my body as part of the treatment plan. In the meantime God was revealing still more about the spiritual warfare I was in and the inner healing I needed. I now understood why God had said, "I am going to heal you from the inside out."

On one of my appointments to the doctor, I asked him if he knew anything about spiritual warfare. "Why?" he asked, "Do you think you're in one?"

"I'm pretty sure," I answered.

He prayed with me and obviously saw some things I didn't yet understand. He wrote down prescriptions he wanted me to get and at the bottom of the list included the name of a book: Deep Wounds, Deep Healing. I ordered the book the very next day. In the meantime I was scheduled to fly to California to meet with another doctor he had recommended.

Ryan planned to fly with me and interview with a company in Los Angeles while we were there. He did not know if we should live in Ohio, Texas, or California, and it was already August and time to register Josh for school. To avoid any more school changes, we decided to homeschool the children.

The book I had ordered came in just before we left for California. I read it as fast as I could and was amazed by what I discovered. God kept revealing more and more about how I needed to be healed. I filled Ryan in on the flight. We arrived at my great aunt's house as the death of Princess Diana was being reported on television. Watching that drama play out there in August of 1997, it seemed to parallel the lack of control we were experiencing in our own lives. It was all very surreal. It felt like our lives had become a drama that we had little say in. Yet, in some ways, we had more say than ever before because every minute of every day we had to choose life and love or bitterness and the death of all we could become.

We met with the doctor. Ryan interviewed with a firm in Los Angeles, and we drove up and down the coast. We also met with our friend Allen Nelson and had a time of prayer. By the end of the prayer, we knew it was time for me and the children to go back to Ohio.

Within a week, all our things in Texas were packed, and I boarded a plane in my wheelchair with two kids, two frogs, and a turtle. The whole adventure hadn't taken one month as we expected, but five months. I wasn't walking, or even sitting up yet, but I could dress myself and take care of my personal hygiene needs with the use of my right arm and the small amount of return I had gained in my left arm. This was a huge improvement. We also knew where we would live and that God had me on an intense inner healing journey. Once again He did the unexpected and somehow managed to disappoint no one.

A Place to Call Home

My people will live in peaceful dwelling places, in secure homes, in undisturbed places of rest.

Isaiah 32:18 (NIV)

We returned to Ohio when that part of the world is in its glory. The sky was cloudless, and the trees were showing off their fall wardrobe. The days were perfect for spending time outside, and so my mother-in-law had taken the kids and me to the park. I was just thinking about how good it felt to be settled at home again when we drove up our driveway and found a brightly-colored notice taped to the garage door. I sat in disbelief. The note stated that this house we were renting was in foreclosure and would be sold at auction in one month. If we couldn't buy the house, we'd have to move out at that time. We went to the auction but were outbid.

We started packing and praying for a new house. Josh was especially disappointed about moving because he loved playing in the creek behind the house. We promptly started praying for a creek at our new house! We were tens of thousands of dollars in debt, had no down payment, and not much time. Ryan started looking for houses and found one he really liked just down the road. He piled us all in the car one day to see if we liked it too. We drove up to the white colonial with black shutters and a red door. "What do you think?" he asked, hoping that we approved.

"It's beautiful," I said, a little stunned. "But how can we afford it?"

Through a series of events, Ryan had already worked out the financing. The kids were excited, so we had Josh go see if anyone still lived there. He looked around for a moment, then came running as fast as he could in the snow, utterly thrilled. He informed us that this was definitely the place God had for us because there was a creek on the property! Josh was right. The house was also vacant, so we were able to buy it below market and with no down payment. To make matters even better, we were able to use the equity we had in the house to take out a second mortgage to consolidate a chunk of our debt. God had provided in more ways than we could have imagined, and He hadn't forgotten a little boy's prayer for a creek!

The first week we were there, Josh came running into the house. "I caught a fish, Mom!"

"With what?" I asked, knowing that we didn't own a fishing pole.

"My hands," he said with excitement. "Pray that I catch more, Mom!"

He ran off and I prayed for fish. A few minutes later he came back even more excited. "When I got back to the creek, there were three fish just waiting for me!"

We were in a sweet season with our Lord. It was the kind of season when prayers are answered quickly and God is moving in plain and obvious ways. Our church was growing and needed money to pay off a new building. Ryan and I prayed and both felt we should give the same amount: an amount we didn't have. I was trying to figure out how much of our pledge we could afford each month as Ryan put the pledge card into the basket. Three days later we got a check in the mail from a church we had belonged to when we had lived in Texas five years before. They were praying for our family and just wanted to bless us. The check was the exact amount we had pledged! We joyfully signed it over to our new church, and a few months later we bought our new home. I have to believe that the pledge money was sort of a spiritual down payment for our own home.

We were blessed to be in a church that truly believed in ministering to one another. The worship was genuine and rich, and the Holy Spirit was welcome. Prayer ministry was offered after each service. We began living for the weekend, waiting to drink from the wells of living water that flowed in that place and from those people. Sometimes, between the suffering and spiritual warfare, we felt beat up and needed other believers to step in and bring us into the presence of God. At the same time, it provided us with an opportunity to minister to others. The church was imperfect like every other, but because people made room for God, He came; and because He came, we never left hurting or hungry.

God used many people at that time to bring us into wholeness. Working through emotional and spiritual healing was as difficult as what I was dealing with physically. On all fronts the issues were inescapable. There was no way to leave them behind for a time and deal with them later. The pain and discomfort were constant. I was dependent on others for the simplest and most basic needs and desires. I had to trust God for everything all day long.

It was far too expensive to have daily outside help, so since I homeschooled the kids, they helped take care of me. Josh had been away from me so much, and now that he had the chance, he stayed very close. I lived on the floor of our living room on a little mat. Josh did all his school work right next to me, and when his work he was finished, he always took Alexa on an adventure in the woods. We got on quite well, all things considered. Friends visited, and they all knew to bring extra clothes for their kids, who inevitably ended up in the creek! When Ryan was home, we were always outside. We went on nearby trails in the Cuyahoga National Forest, drove on what we called "deer runs" to see how many deer we could count in an evening, visited museums and parks, and tried to give the kids as normal a childhood as possible. Even so, the stress of being handicapped or being in a family with a handicapped member is never really left behind. There is always so much more to plan for and consider. Ryan and I both were always exhausted, and even the kids bore a lot on their tiny shoulders.

God always looks out for His children, and in extraordinary circumstances He protects in extraordinary ways. The Lord started showing me in new ways when the kids were getting into trouble. Once they were out sledding, and I "saw" them going down the hill into the creek. Right there on my mat I prayed for God to protect them. I later learned they were using the tree at the bottom to stop themselves! Another time I kept "seeing" Alexa with a bloody face. I thought it was just a scary thought from the enemy. I told my friend Donna who was visiting, and she quickly sent her husband, Jim, to get Alexa. He reported that when he got to the neighbor's house, Alexa was positioned at the top of the slide about to ride down on a skateboard! It took me awhile, but I learned to discern and trust all the different ways God was speaking to me.

It was my nature to be a hands-on mom, but that wasn't possible in my current situation. I wanted to take the children places myself and do the things that moms are supposed to do. As much as I tried to be the kind of mom my kids needed, there were just going to be some glaring insufficiencies. I hated that. I wanted to do more for them but had to realize that God would provide for my kids what I could not. I just hoped that they could see His hand of mercy and love in all of it.

Life on the living room floor wasn't all bad. The kids cuddled with me while they did their school work, and when they went out to play, Chloe, our chocolate lab, took their spot next to me. When Ryan came home, we all ate dinner right there on the living room floor. Friends from church brought meals, helped with laundry, and took the kids and sometimes even me on outings. We experienced a level of community that few modern Americans ever have the opportunity to enjoy. Except for "my room," the house was a disaster. We had no energy to even think about nonessentials. We spent it all on trying to stay in touch with each other, friends, and God. We had been completely stripped to the basics, and that's all that mattered.

In Sickness and in Health

Our marriage went through some interesting changes as well. At first there was a honeymoon period which actually lasted longer than our original one. Then the grace lifted, and all the junk we had before my illness together with the trauma and changes we were trying to deal with now, lay exposed like open, oozing wounds. Just when we were ready to give up, a really good friend stepped in. She called a friend, and they both came over to pray with us. Within an hour the situation looked completely different. It was amazing how quickly God worked when we had people who believed in our marriage help us see through the circumstances. Within weeks we were more in love than we ever had been. We both had lots of "baggage" and really needed something huge to interrupt our lives so God could bring healing. My paralysis provided that opportunity. This whole cycle would play out many times over the years as the Lord dealt with layer after layer of our minds, wills, and emotions. Each time, God's character would be forged in us out of the fires of desperation, and our friendship and intimacy with God and each other would deepen.

Intimacy is an interesting thing. The road to it is not exactly the scenic route, and the process is rather ugly and messy. As a very wise grandmother said to me once, "If two people are going to become one flesh, then some flesh is going to fly!" She was right. The price of true intimacy was the nails that ripped the flesh of Jesus. He paid the price for us to know Him as the lover of our souls, and any earthly relationship that is going to go deep has to be taken to the cross. The trial of my illness gave us two gifts: the opportunity to bond through adversity and a cross on which to nail our flesh.

The hard times were crushing, but the good times were equally intense. I suppose that's how life balances the scales. There is a scene in the movie Toy Story 2 (I practically have that movie memorized thanks to my youngest child) in which the doll Jessie is describing how wonderful it is to be loved by a child. She speaks of being in the child's arms and feeling alive. I always thought of Ryan when I heard that. I would wait for the weekend for him to be home because I never felt sick when I was with him. I was able to do so many normal things when he was around, and he always made me feel beautiful. That's how it is with Jesus. We can do things with Him that are impossible on our own, and even though we are painfully aware of all our flaws, He calls us beautiful.

One day we picked up food at a restaurant, and after we drove home and Ryan parked in the driveway,

I stayed in the car to eat my meal. It was so good just to see the sky and the trees, and sitting in a car was less strain on my body than the wheelchair. Suddenly Ryan jumped in the car, backed up, and parked right in the middle of the front yard!

"What are you doing?" I asked, trying to figure it out.

"I want my little bambina to see the sunset," he announced.

It was an unusually beautiful sunset for that part of the country, but it wasn't enough for my sweet husband to enjoy it himself. He had to find a way to share it with me.

Moments like that kept me going when Ryan did something that made me angry, like the day he came home all excited because, he said, the Lord revealed to him we were moving to North Carolina. We hadn't even been in our new house a year! I had great friends, a wonderful network of people who helped us. The kids were happy, and Ryan's parents were nearby. Besides, we had already moved almost a dozen times in less than ten years. I definitely did not think he was hearing from God and told him so. Within a couple of months, the Lord spoke to me about moving to North Carolina. I had to tell Ryan that he was right.

About the same time, God gave me a strong burden to pray for Josiah, the baby we had been promised. As a family we talked about Josiah often. It gave us so much joy and hope to have such a precious promise. The prayer for Josiah was very focused. I knew I was praying for a particular child who truly existed in the timelessness of God's promise. We believed equally in my healing and in the promise of this child, and in that order. God revealed that there was one small problem. That was not His order. His intention was for the baby to come before the healing! I wish I could say that I said, "Oh, of course, Lord!"

My response was more like Sarah's than Mary's. "You have got to be kidding!" were my exact words. I was appalled that God would suggest such a thing! How much more did He think I could handle? How could I, queen of the living room floor, take care of a baby? And, not that it normally mattered, but what would people think? They would think I had truly lost my mind, and maybe they'd be right!

God knew that a move and a baby were a little too much for me to process at the time, so He pulled out an ever effective parenting tool: distraction. Our friends Steve and Sharon Buie invited us to join them for coffee. That sounded safe enough. Their son James was Josh's age. So we could talk, and the kids could play. They had lived for a year in the former Soviet Union and took teams of short-term missionaries over periodically. Steve began sharing about an upcoming trip to Ukraine. It all sounded wonderful, and then they suggested that we go with them as part of the team. I couldn't believe they were serious, but they were.

I left that day knowing that this was a God thing but also knowing much had to take place to make it happen. I was also beginning to understand that for Christ followers, home was not so much a place to stay, as a place from which to be sent.

To Charlotte via Kharkov

And how will anyone go and tell them without being sent? That is why the Scriptures
say, "How beautiful are the feet of messen-
gers who bring good news!"

Romans 10:15 (NLT)

God knows just how to get us where He wants us. After
all, He originated the art of making the journey just
as significant as the destination. Right after I agreed
that our next move would be to North Carolina, our
friend Mickey Robinson was back in town for a conference. He told us of some very exciting meetings that
he thought we should attend. I wasn't sure if I was up
for traveling, but when he said they were to be held in

Charlotte, North Carolina, I knew we were supposed to go.

That first time we visited North Carolina, we tried to see as many places as possible. We attended the meetings in Charlotte, checked out the beach at Ocean Isle, stopped to have a meal with a high school friend in Raleigh, and then visited more friends in the foothills of Moravian Falls. It was the first of many visits and the introduction to our future home.

During this time, Ryan started looking for a job in Charlotte, and we began praying for the funds to go as a family to Ukraine. As of the week the money was due for the trip, we had only received twenty dollars from the letters we had sent out asking for support. We had no money of our own for this at the time. Ryan had gone on a business trip to Texas when I got a phone call from Colorado and an e-mail from England from people offering to fund our trip. We had gone from no funds for the trip to being completely covered, almost overnight. Ryan, knowing nothing of these developments, called while on a business trip in Houston saying he was really having doubts about going to Ukraine. It wasn't just the money, but the frightening idea of taking two children and a paralyzed wife halfway around the world.

"What would you say if all the money came in?" I asked, knowing that I was setting him up.

"I'd say that it's God, and we'd go," he said, convinced that would never happen.

"Well," I said. "The money came in."

The phone went silent for a long time. After we got off the phone, I got a little nervous myself. This was huge. This was bigger than we could handle alone. This was potentially dangerous. God had spoken clearly by providing the funds, but I really, really needed to know for sure, so I prayed one more time for God to make it clear that we should go.

I fell asleep that same night and dreamed I was eating at a restaurant. My father-in-law, who knew nothing of our plans, was sitting across the table from me. He pointed his finger at me and said, "Go to Ukraine." I woke up immediately. The message was clear.

We spent the next several months on a duel mission: preparing for our trip to Ukraine and trying to find work for Ryan in Charlotte. Ryan had made progress on the job front and interviewed with a small investment banking firm in Charlotte. It looked promising, but the company was slow in responding. In the meanwhile, we were trying to learn a little Russian and also trying to think of everything I would need to be able to make the trip. Most importantly, we tried to prepare spiritually for the trip. One evening as the Ukraine team met for worship and prayer, we were singing about giving our hearts to the Lord. In that moment I heard Him speak to my heart, "No. Give it to them." Then, in a vision, I saw the Lord take my heart, wrap it in the Ukrainian flag and proceed to step on it and crush it until my heart disappeared and became one with the flag. This, He showed me, is the essence of true ministry: a broken heart poured out on others.

The leader of our trip did a phenomenal job of making a way where there seemed to be no way for a woman who happened to be quadriplegic. He had women assigned to help me during the flight as well as while we were there, and everyone helped us keep track of Josh and Alexa, who were eleven and six at the time. It was another beautiful opportunity to experience the community of believers. The flight itself was the most difficult part. It took about twenty-four hours. We stopped in Amsterdam to change planes, and two of the ladies on the team helped me to a bathroom so I could change too. Even healthy people become uncomfortable after twenty hours of travel, but for someone in my condition, it becomes almost unbearable. My bottom was in terrible pain from sitting and getting little circulation, and my left arm ached because it did not have enough muscles or tendons to hold it in its socket. The last leg of the trip was painful to the point of tears. I tried to be tough but just couldn't hold it in anymore.

Thankfully, we arrived in Kiev a short time later. The airport looked like something out of a movie. Everything was old. Once we landed, there was a bit of confusion with me in a wheelchair and two kids in tow. We were unable to stay with the group, and we didn't speak Russian; but once we got through customs and back with our group, it was fine. We all boarded a bus and made it to the hotel. It was great just to lie down in a bed! We spent the next day visiting Kiev. The buildings were painted sky blue and yellow and pink. They were in need of new paint, but they were colorful. The city was beautiful, and we had a great day exploring.

The next morning we were back on the bus for the long ride to Kharkov. Ryan and I sat in the front seat and from there had a great view of the countryside. Rural Eastern Europe is definitely a page out of the history books. The little cottages and old women wearing babushkas made me feel like I'd stepped into a seventeenth-century pastoral painting. In Ukraine they have entire fields of sunflowers whose faces are as big around as dinner plates! It was an absolutely incredible experience for me, and we hadn't really even started yet. The pain of the flight was quickly forgotten as the sheer excitement of being on an adventure took over.

We arrived in Kharkov around midnight and were taken to our apartment. We all experienced a bit of culture shock the first day, but after that even the kids settled into the strange new environment. Sharon and James Buie were our guides on our first outing. The area was mostly residential with many tall gray apartment buildings and some stores. The closest stores were more like snow cone stands in the United States, but had many of the things we have in convenience stores.

We had just been to one of those stores to buy the kids some candy when a young man came up and asked if we spoke English. When he found out we were Americans, he got really excited. He was an American as well! It turned out that he was a Jehovah's Witness missionary. We told him a little about ourselves, and then I asked if we could pray for him right then and there. Although we had very different theological beliefs, God's love was unhindered in reaching the heart of this young man. I really don't think he would have received prayer like that if we had been in America. God is quite amazing! He sent a woman in a wheelchair halfway around the world to pray for a young Jehovah's Witness who lived in her own country!

The following day was Sunday, and we were in for

a treat. These Ukrainian believers held nothing back when it came to worshipping God. We were so blessed! Following the preaching, we Americans split up into teams of two, along with our interpreters, to pray for those who wanted prayer. I think all 500 of them came forward! They were so full of faith and hungry for more of God that it was easy for us to minister. I will never forget these precious people. One very elderly woman touched me deeply. When she came for prayer, the Lord showed me that she had loved and served Him during very difficult times under communism. The Lord told me to thank her on His behalf. I relayed this through the interpreter; and the little old woman began to cry, and then she kissed me. The love of God for this sweet saint was so strong that there was nothing any of us could do except weep.

One of the reasons for this trip was to help with economic development. Although communism had fallen, politically, its ideas were so ingrained in the people that it was hard for them to think outside its confines, especially when it came to finances. Ryan and some of the other men on our team held a conference on finances and then helped those interested to put business plans together. Ryan said what struck him most was that one of the primary goals of each plan was to help feed and clothe others.

Ryan and I were asked to speak at one of the meetings during this conference. I was a little nervous since I was as far from being a business woman as Ukraine is from Texas, but the intercessors insisted that God had showed them that I was to speak as well, so I went. I opened with the disclaimer that I knew nothing about business, but I did know something about having hope in impossible situations. Ryan and I shared many stories, and the Holy Spirit came. I think everyone in that room was crying by the time we finished praying over the people.

We went to the back of the room and sat down next to the pastor, Bill Lynch. Soon after, a Ukrainian soldier entered the room and proceeded to walk up and down the aisles, his black boots clicking on the hard tile floor. As I watched him, I noticed for the first time that the large theatre style curtain hanging to my left had a huge picture of Lenin on it. I nervously asked Bill what the soldier wanted. "He's either looking for someone in particular, or he just wants to know what we're doing here." Bill seemed undisturbed, but I was definitely feeling like I was in another world.

We spent the rest of the afternoon talking via our interpreter, with our new friend Oleg, the man hired to help with me and my wheelchair. We shared what it was like growing up during the Cold War from our different perspectives. I would never have believed as a child that I would grow up to have a former Russian soldier become my friend!

We spent time in the city exploring the artwork and statues and enjoying the culture. Handicapped people are rarely seen there because they are almost always institutionalized, so just being handicapped in that place made a statement. It's not exactly wheelchair friendly either, so it was truly God's grace that my wheels remained intact until we returned to the U.S., at which time one of them completely blew out.

One day Oleg came along with Ryan and I, our

kids, James Buie, and our interpreter for a day of fun for the children. We went to the park, and the kids played on toy cars. We went to the zoo, and then ended the day with two rounds of ice cream at Baskin-Robbins, the nicest, newest building there. The Lord showed up as we shared about His faithfulness. We were all so touched that we ended up crying in our ice cream as the kids chatted happily over theirs. We really didn't want to leave, which is exactly how we felt when it was time to go back to the States. We had only been in Ukraine a little more than two weeks, but it felt like the people had been in our hearts forever.

Once again we boarded for the long bus ride to Kiev from where we would fly back to the States the following morning. The good news was that many of our Ukrainian friends came with us, including Oleg. There in Kiev, on our last night in Ukraine, we celebrated our new found friendships at a beautiful restaurant. Since Oleg, Ryan, and I got lost on the way we were a little late, and all the seats were taken except for a small table for three. Josh and Alexa were sitting together with friends, so the three of us took the small table. The tables were set with gold-plated flatware and regal china covered in royal blue and purple flowers trimmed in gold. Above, the ceiling was covered with royal blue Plexi-glass that was reflective. The atmosphere was charged with the presence of God even as we fellowshipped. We didn't have an interpreter, but we were doing pretty well in spite of that. At one point I answered one of Oleg's questions, and he gave me a very puzzled look. "Why did you say that?" he inquired. I was a little unsure of why he was questioning me, but explained it was in answer to his previous question. He looked at me hard then said in broken English, "Yes, that was my question, but I never spoke it. I only thought it."

The three of us stared at each other in silence. The presence of God became heavy in the room. Many of us began to cry, and I just couldn't stop. Another friend also named Oleg, whom we all referred to as "Little Oleg," went to the piano and began playing "Holy Ground." The glory of God could be seen on our faces. Mine shone so much that a teenage girl on the trip bought a gold-plated bud vase for me to remember the incredible event. We didn't want it to end. Leaving that place and the sweetness of the fellowship was excruciating.

Excruciating in another way would be the well over twenty-four hours of travel that lay ahead of us the next day. The trip proved to be far more physically taxing than the outbound trip had been. At one point on the plane ride, I looked at Ryan and said, "If I can do this, I can have a baby."

I caught a cold on the plane, and within a few days of our return, I had a full-blown case of pneumonia and barely escaped hospitalization. It was a difficult time for us. We missed our Ukrainian friends and their enormous faith. We remembered them every time we ate, and wondered if they had enough food. Our hearts had been softened and stretched. We cried every day for weeks.

At the same time, Ryan got word from his placement firm that the company he felt sure was God's will for him had not given him the job. It didn't seem possible. Ryan so definitely believed he had heard otherwise from the Lord. He called the president of the company himself, got the job, and three weeks later we moved to Charlotte, North Carolina.

Promises, Promises!

Just before we left Ohio, God gave us a series of promises to take with us. One night we attended a packed-out meeting at our church where a guest minister was speaking. He finished his sermon and looked my way. He stared as if he were seeing something in my eyes, and then he spoke: "The Lord is going to heal you," he started. The crowd erupted in praise. When there was a lull, he finished by declaring, "What Satan has meant for evil, God will use for good!" The crowd settled down a long time before I did. I was so glad that my friends who had prayed for me for so long got to hear for themselves what God had been speaking to me all along. The guest minister also made a reference to the baby! I went home and called my mom to tell her what had happened. Then Ryan and I settled in for the night. I awakened him early the next morning.

"Ry," I whispered.

"Hmm." He didn't open his eyes.

"I had a vision in my dream last night," I continued.

"You had a what in your where?" he asked with eyes half open now.

"I dreamed I was looking at an empty baby crib, and then all of a sudden I had a vision of Josiah. He was only a few weeks old, and he was adorable! In the dream I kept saying to myself, 'Don't blink. Don't blink. Because when you do you won't get to see him for a long time.'"

Ryan was awake and up on one arm now. "What did he look like?" he asked.

"He looked like one of ours, with blond hair and blue eyes, but he definitely looked different than Josh or Alexa. He was just so cute, Honey!"

"Wow!" was all he could say.

Just before we moved to North Carolina, we celebrated Josh's and Alexa's birthdays with their Ohio friends for the last time. Josh had a slumber party. I learned the year before that boys that age never sleep at overnight parties, so my friend Eileen invited me to sleep at her house. It was a bit challenging getting me into the house because there were steps we couldn't navigate with the wheelchair. Eileen's husband Frank was already asleep, and we hated to wake him. Besides, I think we had more fun doing it on our own. We managed to get me out of my wheelchair and onto the steps, and Eileen pulled me from there into the house. Then I held onto her ankle, and she dragged me through the kitchen into the living room where she set me up for the night. I honestly don't know how Frank slept through all the giggling! The next morning as Eileen and I were chatting, Frank came down the stairs.

"You know," he said after greeting me, "I had a dream about you last night."

"Really?" I asked, very interested.

"Yes," he answered. "You were pregnant with Josiah. It won't be long," he added knowingly. Frank and Eileen had believed with us for Josiah for several years, and the encouragement that he would come soon gave me hope.

I knew with the heartbreak of leaving our friends and family the Lord was helping me to stay focused on what He had for us in the future. Otherwise it would have been too easy to give into the temptation to look back. My mom came to help us move. The day before we left, we had a combination birthday party for Alexa and going-away party for ourselves. More than fifty people came to see us off. The next morning we packed me, the kids, the dog, and the cat into the car and cried all the way out of Ohio.

Miracles Happen

Blessed is she who believed that what the
LORD has said to her will be accomplished!
Luke 1:45 (NIV)

Sometimes I don't realize how much prayer is going
into something until the prayer burden is lifted. So
much energy went into our trip to Ukraine and our
move to North Carolina, that once those events took
place, I had an empty, unsettled feeling. We moved
into our new apartment and got Josh into a new school.
Alexa was still homeschooled. The kids loved the warm
weather, and swimming in October was a real treat; but
I felt something was missing. I definitely missed my

friends, but that didn't explain the nagging feeling in my spirit.

"I think I'm bored," I confessed to Ryan in the car one day.

"Why are you bored?" he asked.

"I don't know," I pondered. "I think God needs to give me a new assignment." We were in a new city and a new church, making new friends, but something still wasn't right.

A few weeks later I had another dream about Josiah. In the dream he was about nine-months-old, sitting on my lap and very chubby. A voice behind me spoke. Three times it was repeated, "Raise him as an intercessor!" After the third time, I kissed him on the cheek and said, "Yes! And he won't be happy until he dances."

It was such an incredible dream, and I was thrilled to see him again; but it left me with the kind of empty ache that only women who have longed to hold their children know. A few days later, I found myself running out of grace.

"Ryan, I just can't take this anymore! God has spoken that I will be healed and that I will have Josiah, but it is just too hard to hold on to both these promises any longer. God needs to either heal me or give us Josiah!" I was feeling my lack of control to bring about what God had spoken, yet He was still quite in control. He had moved me from the point of arguing about having a baby while paralyzed to declaring it needed to happen right now! God had me speaking His will out of my own mouth, and I was the one thinking that He needed to get on the ball! He truly understands that we are but dust!

The next weekend we took Josh and Alexa to see a movie. I was watching previews when one came on showing a man changing a baby boy's diaper. The baby peed like a fountain, and the man was scrambling to take care of the situation. It was supposed to be humorous, and to most people it was. I, however, burst into tears! My first thought was, "I've gone crazy!" My second thought was, "I'm pregnant!"

I told Ryan what had happened and that he should buy a pregnancy test. He looked at me as if I were crazy, but I insisted. He decided it was easier to comply than argue with a crazy woman. I took the test, and just as I suspected, it was positive.

I went to bed that night terrified. Suddenly, the reality of what was occurring hit me. After all, I could only move my head and right arm, and the thought of taking care of an infant seemed monumental. The prophecies and dreams were all forgotten as I realized we'd just jumped off the cliff of faith into the great unknown of God's will. Ryan spent the next few days reassuring me that this would all turn out okay. Once I got over the initial fear, we began telling our friends who had been praying about Josiah for years. Their excitement and faith boosted mine, and I was able to focus on the baby rather than my own uncertainties. Alexa was so excited to have a baby "of her own" that she could hardly stand the thought of having to wait nine long months. Josh was excited, too, but wanted to be certain that it "wasn't another sister." The early part of the pregnancy moved along without much excitement. I was really tired and really hungry, and everything seemed normal, that is for a pregnant quadriplegic.

I did notice something rather unusual about six weeks into the pregnancy. There was something under my skin on the left side of my abdomen near my hip bone. I showed Ryan and Alexa, and we watched as it grew bigger almost daily. I called a friend who is a midwife's assistant, and asked if that could be the baby. She said it couldn't be since the uterus would not be big enough yet to stretch to the hip. It made sense to me, but since there was no other explanation for this little, caterpillar-like growth, I couldn't help but wonder.

Toward the end of the first trimester I caught a cold that I couldn't shake. Ryan got worried and insisted I see a doctor. The doctor was very friendly and quite interested in how I had become paralyzed. I told him I was pregnant, and he became very interested in that as well.

"That's great!" he said. Then looking at Ryan, he asked, "Were you there for the insemination?"

Ryan didn't quite get the question so I jumped in for him.

"Oh, he was there all right," I grinned, giving the doctor just enough rope to hang himself.

"Well, how was the insemination done?" he asked, expecting to hear some medical explanation.

"The old fashioned way," I quipped.

It took him a minute, but he finally caught on, at which point I assured him that he had just won a spot in the book I planned to write.

After Christmas, around the third month of the pregnancy, we took the whole family, including my mom, to hear the baby's heartbeat. At first Ryan and I were the only ones in the room as the technician tried to find the heartbeat. She tried and tried, but no heartbeat could be found. After many attempts, Ryan and I shot each other nervous glances. Something wasn't right. This could not be happening! God had promised! He had given us dreams and prophecies! My heart was racing.

"Wait!" I blurted out before anyone could give up. "Could you try listening over here, next to my hipbone?" I pointed to the spot where the little, oblong lump had been growing. The technician looked at me for a moment, then did as I requested. The next thing we heard was the rapid, "swish, swish, swish" of our tiny baby's heartbeat.

"There he is!" I announced triumphantly. We all had tears in our eyes by now. We called in the rest of the family to hear Josiah's heartbeat and celebrate his life.

It seems that the curvature in my spine coupled with the paralysis caused my uterus to shift to the left. Knowing this made us realize what a very slim chance I actually had to become pregnant. It was a miracle in every way.

Miracles are tricky things. Most of us have prayed for one at some point in our lives. Only those who have lived them understand the cost. Yes, Jesus paid the real price with His sacrifice on the cross, but for the things of heaven to intersect the space of earth, someone must take up his or her own cross and follow Christ's example.

One Sunday morning in particular, I felt the cost weighing on me. My body felt too weak to even lie still. I so wanted to go to church to worship the Lord and be in His presence, but getting dressed was such a monumental task. First I cried. Then I cried out, "Lord, if I go to church today, will you please show up for me?" I couldn't bear the thought of going to church that day and not having a real encounter with the God I so desperately needed. I went and He came! I cried all through worship, just out of joy that He was there in such a tangible way. "Lord," I called out silently, "when are you going to heal me?" I'd asked that question a thousand times and never received a straight answer. This time He answered with a question.

"Didn't I promise you a good husband?" I looked over at Ryan worshipping with His whole heart, unaware the he was the center of a conversation.

"Yes, Lord."

"And didn't I give you one?"

"Yes, Lord." I smiled at His faithfulness.

"And didn't I promise you another baby?"

"Yes, Lord, you did."

"And didn't I give you one?"

"Yes, Lord," I said, smiling more now and patting my tummy.

"And haven't I promised that I would heal you?"

"Yes, Lord," I answered, feeling a little ashamed for even questioning such a faithful friend.

"I AM the promise keeper," he said, and then ended the conversation with this, "and thank you for carrying Josiah."

I was undone once again by His incredible love and left wondering about His ways.

The pregnancy wasn't as difficult as I feared it

might be, but it did have its unique challenges. I was unable to get myself in and out of bed without a big tummy let alone with one, so things did get comical. When Ryan wasn't there to help me, Alexa would sort of shove me, and I would use a board designed to move people in and out of wheelchairs to scoot across the bed on my tummy. This was what I called "bed surfing," and at the time of this writing, it is still the method I use to get into bed.

Alexa became my helper in so many ways. She changed my sheets and clothes and did just about anything I needed, even though she was only seven. Her servant's heart coupled with the excitement of having a baby coming made her the perfect helper. When we named her, I had no idea how appropriate it was. Her name means "helper and defender of mankind."

One day I had to ask her to put my socks on. Getting socks on my feet is harder than trying to put socks on a baby because my feet are bigger and somewhat floppy. As she struggled to accomplish the task, I told her that one day in heaven Jesus was going to say to her, "Thank you, Alexa, for putting my socks on me!"

She thought that was rather silly, then I told her that Jesus once said, "I tell you the truth, whatever you did for one of the least of these brothers of mine, you did for me" (Matthew 25:40). Her eyes lit up, and the next day she asked if she could put my socks on me again.

As the pregnancy progressed and the baby grew, it was becoming more apparent that our lives would never be the same. We had just settled into some sort of rhythm in our very abnormal lives, and now a baby would come; and everyone knows that there is no normal with babies around, even if you aren't paralyzed. With that in mind, Ryan and I decided to incorporate the baby's sonogram with a weekend getaway. Those of you who are parents know that anything can be romantic if the kids are gone.

Instead of going to the hospital down the street, we drove two and a half hours to a hospital in Asheville and stayed at a lovely bed and breakfast whose claim to fame was that Robin Williams stayed there while filming Patch Adams. I love that movie, so it worked for me.

The sonogram technicians showed us the baby and let us know that everything looked normal. Then she told us it was a girl! I couldn't believe it. Worried she might be right, I started praying for clarity. Just then the baby moved, and any confusion was immediately cleared up. There was no denying that this baby was our Josiah Storm! With our concerns put to rest, Ryan and I enjoyed what would be our last moments without children for the next four years.

Detour

As the time of the birth drew near, I assembled my birthing team for a home birth. We had a nanny, two midwives, and enlisted the help of prayer teams both at the birth and at a distance. It didn't exactly go as planned. After several hours of pushing, the baby's heartbeat started to drop. It was time for Plan B.

They carried me to the car, and we all raced to the hospital, which was only a few minutes from our apartment. When we got there, the baby was crowning. I was rushed into a delivery room and put on the bed. The nurse bent my legs so I could hold onto them as I pushed with all my might. After a few minutes, Josiah Storm was born.

I was so relieved until I noticed that he was blue and lifeless. The nurses scooped him up and gave him oxygen right away. He pinked up quickly and was taken to the neonatal unit where they placed him on a ventilator, inserted a catheter and feeding tube, and attached him to monitors. His APGAR score (a number from one to ten given to all newborns rating their health) was a one, meaning that his survival expectancy was almost nonexistent.

It was three in the morning. Ryan was an absolute wreck, and I felt guilty because I felt so much better now that I was no longer pregnant. There was no way we could sleep. As soon as it was morning, I started calling my prayer chain. Margot was my Midwest connection. Lynne had me covered on the East Coast. My mom had Texas, and I called my friend AJ in California. Each of them had a group of people praying.

We all kept praying nonstop. The first visitor was the chaplain. She was no ordinary hospital chaplain. It was her first day on the job and an absolute divine appointment. By the end of the prayer I was declaring that Josiah would breathe "this day!"

"This day" would prove to be one of the longest of my life. It had been almost eight hours since his birth, and I still hadn't been able to see my baby. The nurses tried to get me up in my wheelchair, but my blood pressure plummeted. The bottom number was in the thirties! I went back to bed frustrated and discouraged, still longing to hold this long-awaited baby.

Ryan gave me reports about how cute he was as the doctor started running tests on him. A nurse went over to the neonatal nursery and took a couple of Polaroids. He was cute! He looked just like he did in the first dream I had of him, except that now he had a bruise on the left side of his forehead. Again it seems that my scoliosis was the culprit. The result caused him to shift too far to the left while I was trying to push him through the birth canal, and his head kept hitting my pelvic bone.

The doctor came and spoke to us. The tests on his lungs had come back great. There was not a thing wrong with his lungs and therefore no real explanation as to why he wasn't breathing. We just had to wait to see if he would start breathing on his own.

Finally, my nurse found a gurney. Sitting up with my head and legs supported, I was wheeled to the neonatal unit to meet my son. I rolled past the tiniest people I had ever seen in my life. Josiah was the only one on life support, but he looked like the most unlikely candidate there. Even though he was one month premature, he weighed in at a healthy six pounds and fourteen ounces. Compared to his nursery mates, he appeared huge! I peered down at him amidst all the wires, tubes, and noisy machines keeping him alive and spoke for the first time to this long-awaited miracle.

"Josiah," I whispered, "Mommy is here now. Everything is okay. Mommy is with you, and it's okay to breathe now." I stayed as long as I was permitted, then uncurled his tiny hand from my finger and was taken back to my room.

My heart sank. I just wanted to hold him. In the afternoon the doctor returned. He was at a loss. There was no physical reason that this child still hadn't breathed. Ryan suggested that maybe he was too exhausted. The doctor suggested that maybe he had brain damage. I liked Ryan's idea better.

That was it for me! I hadn't slept in thirty hours. I had just given birth, and now this guy was telling me my baby's brain was damaged! As soon as he left the room, I started making phone calls to the prayer team again. Then I got a call from Barbara, who was looking after Josh. She said he seemed very anxious and wanted to see me. I hadn't even had a chance to think about Josh and Alexa yet. Barbara asked if she could bring him to the hospital. As soon as Josh saw me and saw that I was fine, he said, "I want to see the baby!"

Ryan took Josh over to meet his brother. He came back to tell me goodbye, happy and excited. "Oh, Mom, the baby looks so big and healthy!" As he said good-bye, I told him, "Don't worry about your brother, Josh. He's a tough little guy."

Ryan returned from the nursery with confusing news. He had been asked to hold Josiah's arms down while the nurse gave him a shot of morphine. The nurse said they didn't want him to be in pain, but just how did they know he was in pain? Was such a power-ful drug really necessary? I wasn't getting any answers. Ryan left the hospital to hear God clearly.

We've Turned the Corner!

Ryan went to a Wendy's restaurant to pray. He came back with a full stomach and a word from God. "Kelly," he said with a confidence that had been missing since Josiah's birth, "the Lord says we've turned the corner!" He then went down the hall to meet with a colleague to take care of some business regarding a deal they were working on at the bank.

I knew I needed more reinforcements for this battle. I called my friend Eileen and told her the latest. She asked her husband, Frank (who before we even left Ohio had dreamt I was pregnant with Josiah), to get on the phone too. When he finished praying, he said, "Kelly, I know that God just touched that boy. I felt the anointing leave me."

Frank is no stranger to God's power. I trusted what he said. Before I had a chance to process it though, two nurses came in to tend to me. A few minutes later, another nurse came in. She had long, blond hair with bangs and wore a colorful scrub shirt like all the other neonatal nurses. She looked at me and announced, "Hi! I'm Catherine from neonatal." She was pleasant and upbeat. She acted as if I should know her. "I said I would come if anything happened either way," she finally said.

My mind raced, trying to remember if I had met her. Had she met Ryan, possibly? Then suddenly her words registered. "Wait! What happened either way?" I questioned.

"The baby pulled out his tubes and has been breathing on his own for five minutes."

"Praise God!" I cried out. Then I looked at Catherine and said through my tears, "Can I hug you?" She smiled and came over for a hug. Then she stepped back and said, "The next half hour is very important. If we get him through that, we'll be home free."

I thanked her and she left. The other two nurses finished up and left too. I grabbed the phone to call Ryan, but he had left his cell phone in my room. I called my mom, Margot, and Eileen, who all called others. Everyone was worshipping and praising God!

Finally Ryan came back, and I shared the incredible news with him. He sank into the chair and cried and thanked God. I waited until the thirty minutes passed and then called the nursery to check on Josiah. I was told that his nurse was working on him and that she would come as soon as possible.

We waited, expecting to see Catherine any minute. Finally, the door opened. A neonatal nurse came in and sat next to us. Her cropped brown hair matched the shortness in her demeanor. She spoke of Josiah in only clinical terms and added, "Don't get too excited. Sometimes babies like this forget to breathe in the night, so we may have to put him back on oxygen."

Too late, I thought. I'm already so excited that someone is going to have to peel me off this ceiling! Then I blurted out, "Wait a minute! His nurse, Catherine, said if we got him past the first thirty minutes we'd be home free!"

She bristled and said curtly, "I'm his nurse, and I don't know who Catherine is or anything about thirty minutes."

I knew better than to say another word, but the fact that she didn't even know Catherine more than piqued my curiosity. I asked everyone I saw for the next four days, and no one knew of a Catherine in neonatal or even a nurse that fit her description!

Ryan stayed the rest of that day and night with us in the hospital. At five the next morning, he went across the hall to see how Josiah had fared through the night. He stepped into the dimly lit nursery and saw, a few yards away, a single light illuminating Josiah's bed with his doctor leaning over him. As he approached, the doctor turned to Ryan and declared with confidence, "Well, it looks like we've turned the corner!"

He had just uttered the exact words the Lord spoke to Ryan the afternoon before. The fact that a newborn baby, less than a day old, pulled out his ventilator while on morphine and began breathing on his own for the first time still overwhelms me every time I think about it. What an awesome God!

Everything in me wanted to see our miracle for myself. I used the electronic hospital bed as a tilt table to get my body accustomed to sitting up again. My hope was that this would help my blood pressure remain high enough to allow me to sit in my wheelchair. My body was so exhausted that it took every ounce of energy I had to try to sit up. I know for certain that nothing but pure maternal determination kept me going. My hard work paid off. I successfully sat in my wheelchair that morning and went to the nursery to see my baby. Ryan and my friend Lisa came with me. A couple of the nurses came over to Josiah's crib to greet us. He looked so much better without the ventilator. He still had lots of other wires and tubes, but he was breathing on his own. One of the nurses asked if I wanted to hold him. "Are you kidding?" I asked. I couldn't believe it. I had waited six years and two very long days to hold this baby. When he was put in my arms, it was a fulfillment of God's promise and the answer to many prayers.

Other people from our church came to pray for him. The nurses cautioned us that he might still have problems and would very likely have cerebral palsy. We continued to pray and believe that this would not be the case.

Alexa met her brother that same afternoon. As soon as she saw him she said, "He has Dad's chest," which he does, but I thought it was a funny way for such a little girl to greet her new brother.

Josiah did such a good job nursing that the feeding tube was removed, then the catheter as well. Finally, he joined the rest of the babies in the main section of the neonatal unit in a little basinet. His siblings could now hold him too. Josh didn't want him to feel alone, so he bought him a Curious George doll to sleep beside him.

I gave birth on Monday, and the doctor released me from the hospital on Thursday. Josiah couldn't leave because he had jaundice and needed treatment. I cried all the way home. The next morning I called the neonatal unit to check on him and ask them not to feed him because I was on my way. The whole family went to the hospital. I fed him, and everyone took turns rocking him. Afterwards, we went out to eat then went home to rest with plans to return to the hospital in the afternoon.

Taking Home a Miracle

Right after we got home, the hospital called with good news. The doctor had checked on Josiah and was ready to release him three days earlier than expected. We were elated! We piled back into the car and headed to the hospital. A nurse greeted us warmly. She spoke for many of the nurses who were amazed that we were leaving with a healthy baby. "Well, you're taking home our miracle boy!" she exclaimed.

"Yes I am!" I smiled.

We stayed to have pictures taken then brought Josiah to his new home. Bringing Josiah home marked a huge victory in so many ways. To receive a promise from God in the most impossible of circumstances, have it confirmed, and then persevere in prayer through so many obstacles and battles was miracle enough. But to have the privilege of physically birthing that promise in the form of a beautiful baby, and in my condition, is almost too incredible to put into words. We all knew that this little boy came to earth as a physical, tangible representation of the hope God had given us for my complete healing. If we were ever to have reason to trust God and His Word, now was the time.

However, as I had already learned, living in the miraculous tends to be very costly. We successfully got Josiah home, but now we had to figure out how to take care of him, twelve-year-old Joshua, seven-year-old Alexa, and me. Ryan and I were beyond exhausted by the time we all got to bed that night. I had to let Ryan sleep because I would need him so much the next day. We had a special three-sided bed which was attached to ours so I could reach Josiah myself. When he woke up the first night, I didn't quite have it down how to get him changed on my own. I felt so guilty, but decided to wake Alexa at two in the morning to ask for help. She was sleeping on the floor next to my bed because she didn't want to be away from her new brother. I whispered her name and asked if she minded helping with the baby. She popped up immediately saying, "I get to help?"

The next day was a Sunday, and we desperately needed help, so we phoned a friend who had recently e-mailed and said to call if we needed anything. We were about to test how sincere that offer had been! She and her husband packed up their kids and drove almost four hours to rescue us. They blessed us beyond belief, staying until my mom arrived a few days later, who then helped us through the next couple of weeks.

The first three months with a new baby can exhaust the strongest of parents. We were not the strongest of parents. Even with a part-time nanny, there were times that it seemed so exhausting and logistically maddening that I wondered why we had done this to ourselves. Then the Lord would remind me that this truly was His doing. In those moments I was more overwhelmed by the awesome goodness of God than the difficulty of the situation.

One time Alexa and I sat staring in wonder at Josiah. "Sometimes I just can't believe he's really here, Mom."

"I know. Me too," I agreed.

"He's just so cute!"

I agreed that he was absolutely beautiful. We just

kept staring in awe that God had answered our prayers in such a precious way.

"Thanks, Mom," Alexa said after a long silence.

"For what?" I asked.

"For having the baby," she answered as if it were obvious.

I just looked at her in amazement. "You're welcome," I said hesitantly, knowing that I could take little credit for the miracle before us, yet knowing what she meant. There are rarely miracles without humans willing to lay down their lives in some way and partner with God. It's a mystery, but that is how God works: through people.

Under His Protection

His huge outstretched arms protect you—
under them you're perfectly safe; his arms
fend off all harm.

Psalm 91:4 (Msg)

God works through all kinds of people. Sometimes He uses people as instruments of divine intervention without them realizing it. As an investment banker, Ryan often travels, and it's common for him to fly to New York City for business. When Josiah was three-months-old, Ryan had a client in Utah who hired him to sell their company. He had a potential buyer in New York City at a company called Cantor Fitzgerald. Ryan and the Utah clients had scheduled a meeting on Monday morning, September 10, 2001, which meant he had to fly out Sunday afternoon. Right before he left, he said something that turned out to be an ominous foreshadowing: "These guys at Cantor Fitzgerald aren't calling me back all of a sudden. It's like they've fallen off the face of the earth!"

We had gone to church that Sunday, and, for some reason, I felt Ryan should get prayer before he flew out. He did and departed as planned. The next day he met with his clients in midtown Manhattan. Over lunch, the clients requested he join them for a nine o'clock meeting the next morning at the Merrill Lynch offices in the World Trade Center. He agreed since he had to go to another meeting across the street and could set that appointment for 8 A.M. He called Barry, his assistant in Charlotte, and asked him to set it up. He was still eating lunch when Barry called to tell him he had made the appointment for 1:30 that day, September 10, instead of the following morning, September 11.

Frustrated that Barry hadn't followed his instructions, but now having no choice, Ryan and his clients cut short their lunch and caught a cab back to the business district for the meeting. On the ride over, Ryan told his clients that since the meeting time had changed and he was not a key player in the Merrill Lynch deal, he didn't really need to stay over and would just get a flight back to Charlotte that night. He called me that evening while I was grocery shopping on the Internet with Josiah strapped to my chest in a front pack. "Pray I get out of here tonight," he said. "It's the last flight out. It's raining hard, and if I don't get out now, I'll be stuck here."

He made it out and got home around midnight. The next morning, he was on his way to his Charlotte office as usual when the first plane crashed into the World Trade Center. I fielded a lot of calls that day from people wondering if Ryan was still in New York. We were shaken to the core as we realized that he narrowly escaped possible death.

We watched CNN in shock as the president and c.e.o. of Cantor Fitzgerald, the company that Ryan had intended to meet with, was interviewed and told reporters that his entire staff had perished in the attack. A few days later Ryan appeared visibly shaken. "Are you okay?" I asked just to give him an opportunity to unload.

"I checked my messages for the first time today," he began. "The guys' voices from Cantor Fitzgerald were still on my machine, and none of them are alive. Then I realized that there were documents sitting on their desks with my signature on them that don't even exist anymore, and I don't know what happened to my clients from Utah."

We were both rendered speechless, so we just held each other for a long time. The next day Ryan received a call from his Utah clients. They had been in the World Trade Center when the first plane hit. The person they were meeting with had survived the bombing in 1993 and took no chances waiting around. They all escaped the building before it collapsed and were driving back to Utah in a rental car when they called.

All Things Work Together

We had been living in an apartment for over a year waiting for our house in Ohio to sell. We thought that after September 11, it might not sell for a long time to come. The events of September 11, however, were exactly what sold our house. A family living in a pricey neighborhood near our previous home in Ohio was influenced by the tragedy to make a lifestyle change. They sold their home. The wife quit her job, and they lowered their costs by purchasing our place. This allowed us to purchase land and build a home. Because we got such a good deal on the land, we had equity in the house as soon as we bought it. We were able to take out a home equity loan and pay off the high-interest debt we had been carrying since I became ill. The home equity loan was paid off quickly, and for the first time in years, we had financial breathing room.

I don't even pretend to understand why things happen the way they do. I don't know why some people live and others die. I don't know why some are healed and others are not. I only know that God is sovereign and that His character is unchanging and He is worthy of my worship and allegiance no matter what.

Waiting on the Promises

But they that wait upon the LORD shall renew their strength; they shall mount up with wings as eagles; they shall run, and not be weary; and they shall walk, and not faint.

Isaiah 40:31 (KJV)

The exact distance between the promise and the Promised Land is always way too long. It is in this in-between time that we have some of the greatest opportunities that we will ever be presented. We will never understand faith and hope unless we are in a hopeless situation that requires great faith. We will never understand the peace that passes understanding until life seems out of control. And we will never learn to overcome until we're forced to fight.

When I was first placed in ICU, a lady from our church stayed with me while Ryan made arrangements for the children. I remember telling her not to worry because, "This isn't the worst thing that's ever happened to me." I wasn't exaggerating. Even near death, I realized I'd been through worse and had been blessed with the opportunity to witness God's faithfulness every time. I knew that He would be with me this time too.

I also knew that God doesn't do things exactly as I would. He is faithful to His Word, but He does not live in the box that we sometimes create with His Word. Often He purposely allows things that crush our human ideas and doctrines because He so desperately longs for us to know Him for who He really is.

The God we serve is just that good! He will patiently wait years to bring about not only His plan but also the intimacy He desires with each of us. His patience cannot be exaggerated. We are impatient because we are bound by time. When God forces us to wait, He helps us gain an eternal perspective. In the light of eternity, what's a decade or so?

It's been almost thirteen years since that life-changing day in Pelham Manor, New York. Every day is difficult, some more so than others. Sometimes Ryan and I are doing great, and sometimes we're angry, sad, or overwhelmed. Always we are exhausted. But life is hard for most people I know! We are not the only ones with challenges. Ours are just more obvious.

Probably the hardest part for me, as a mom, is seeing the effect on my kids. I've had to learn to trust God with their lives, as well as my own. As hard as it is, all of us parents have to watch our kids go through pain and know they will have to find their own way just as we do.

On top of my paralysis, we as a family still have all the usual challenges that come with marriage, kids, finances, and daily life. Believe me, we aren't one of those families who will send you holiday newsletters of glowing reports. We're more likely to e-mail an S.O.S. and then call you with the report of how God answered our prayers in spite of ourselves.

I've come to truly understand that, "Man does not live on bread alone but by every word that comes out of the mouth of God" (Deuteronomy 8:3, NIV). I don't know what I would do if I couldn't hear God's voice through His Scripture, in my heart, and through other believers. I have learned to depend on what God says and not on what I see or how I feel.

People sometimes ask if I ever doubt or want to give up. I've had doubts come my way, but I just can't bring myself to accept them. I think of the price Jesus paid for healing and of how much more He suffered than I will ever comprehend, and I know that He deserves everything He paid for. Far be it from me that my unbelief should ever cause one stripe on His back to have been taken in vain! He paid the price for my healing; therefore, the very least I should do is believe.

I once had a friend who was dying. He told me he didn't have the faith to believe for his healing. I don't think there is any shame in that. It was time for him to go home, and he knew it. I'm a little jealous he got there before me! I've been near death, and it's hard to want to be here if you get even a glimpse of the other side. It takes enormous faith to both live and die gracefully.

God's plans are not dependent on our circumstances. When He calls us to a purpose, nothing can stop Him fulfilling it if we continue to trust Him. We may need to adjust the way we go about it, and the road we have to take may lead us to places we never dreamed we'd travel, but in the end we will live out our destiny if we remain steadfast.

I have found that God's plans almost always take longer to unfold than I ever hoped and almost never in the way I imagined. It takes faith to wait, but at the same time, truly waiting on God ignites real faith. The art of waiting, of finding the secret place where you abide and commune with Him in the midst of every circumstance, will cause you to be more than an overcomer. It is in that place of intimacy that miracles and destinies are nurtured. It is in that place where you find the strength to run and not grow weary. It is in that place where you find the courage to walk it out.

Epilogue

At the time of this writing, I am still making progress which baffles the medical community. I don't pass out anymore, and my neurological system has healed to the point that bumping my wheelchair doesn't feel like an earthquake in my bones. I have a long way to go, but I am officially no longer paralyzed from the neck down on the left and from the chest down on the right. I am one of very few people who can say I was once a quadriplegic. I have the sensation of touch and pressure all the way to my toes, and the sensations of heat, cold, and pain are returning. I have use of my left arm and hand but need much more therapy to regain strength and full use. I have remarkable return of movement in my torso, and recently, for the first time in twelve years,

I was able to meet my goals in physical and occupational therapy. I've been driving for three years, which is a huge accomplishment as well as an enormous freedom. The thing that amazes those in the medical field most is that I continue to improve year after year, and I never regress. There are no plateaus in the spirit. We go on from glory to glory. And speaking of glory, may God get all of it!

I will continue working hard and believing for all that God has promised. I have no reason to believe anything less! Please pray with me and follow my progress on my website www.livingthecall.com.